Profits Pending

How Life Patents Represent the Biggest Swindle of the 21st Century

Matthew Albright

D1275033

Common Courage Press   Monroe, Maine

ISBN: 1-56751-230-5 paper
ISBN: 1-56751-231-3 cloth

Library of Congress Cataloging-in-Publication Data is
available on request from the publisher

Common Courage Press
Box 702
Monroe, ME 04951

800-497-3207

FAX (207) 525-3068
orders-info@commoncouragepress.com

See our website for e versions of this book.
www.commoncouragepress.com

First Printing
Printed in Canada

For James N. Albright, Scientist and Father

Acknowledgements

I am deeply indebted to Martin Teitel who sent me off on this project and then made sure I did not go too far adrift. This book owes its existence to his friendship, guidance, and support. Kimberly A.Wilson's "no patents on life" work at the Council for Responsible Genetics gave me a solid foundation from which to build. The staff at CRG—Sophie Kolehmainen, J.D. Suzanne C. Theberge and Susan Fasten—read and reread the manuscript in all of its many forms and provided much needed laughs, Chinese food, and beer. Thanks as well to the CRG board members who gave me feedback, especially Ruth Hubbard, whose close reading was invaluable. Greg Bates at Common Courage Press always had faith in the project and helped shape it into readable form. It is important to note that while these individuals and CRG assisted in many ways, the responsibility for this manuscript, the ideas and opinions herein, and any errors that might have inadvertently crept in, rest solely with the author.

The staff, faculty, and programs at Harvard Divinity School, especially Dudley Rose and the Office of Ministerial Studies, allowed me the time for research and provided an excellent arena for thoughtful debate. The guidance of Professor Kimberley Patton was essential. A special thanks also goes out to all my friends and members of my family who have supported this project with patience and companionship, as well as with fierce debate.

As evidenced by the footnotes and references, this project owes a great deal to the many scientists and reporters whose extensive studies and continuing investigative work expose the effects of life patents.

Contents

Foreword

Bill McKibben

If you wanted to list the most important technological developments of human history, the top two items might well be the discovery of fire, and the emerging ability to manipulate genes. Fire changed the world, made us a new species; we feel the aftershocks of that discovery even today, in the industrialization that marks our age. Now genetic manipulation offers a tool at least as powerful—offers the prospect of change so fundamental we can only begin to guess at the consequences.

And yet, oddly, we don't much seem to care. Sure, we can muster a few days of interest for Dolly the doppelganger sheep, but in general we leave this question to the scientists, and to their entrepreneurial colleagues intent on turning research into product. This is one of the few great issues of our time and yet the debate about its potential has barely been engaged, at least in this nation. It's as if we split the atom and no one had cared, no one had stepped forward to carry on the decades-long debate that brought us back from the nuclear brink and yet helped figure out those areas (medicine, for instance) where it made sense to use the atom.

There are two ways to duck this issue, and we are taking both of them. One is to pretend that it's nothing new, just the natural extension of the cross-breeding humans have practiced since the start of agriculture. This is nonsense—nature confined such experimentation to very strict boundaries. A pea and a pig couldn't mate, nor a person with either of them, so their genes were forever separate. In a way, that was what defined the "nature" of any species. Now, if we choose, there are no such boundaries.

The other way to ignore the implications of this question is to insist that nothing could possibly be done to alter the future development of this technology. That too is nonsense. A great deal of the research, for instance, is driven mainly by economics, dependent on the prospects of huge markets for patented forms of life. The European Parliament has taken steps toward banning patents; were the U.S. and Japan to consider similar restrictions, the chances that we'd be patenting the genetic code of New Guinean tribals would decrease; the future would change. There are many other possible forks in this road as well, just as at one time we could have dealt with the invention of the car in a different, more productive fashion.

The list of reasons to be apprehensive about genetic engineering is long. There are the physical fears about the dangers inherent in monocultures or in manipulated genes crossing to wild populations, the social fears about how this will likely accelerate the differences between the rich and the poor parts of the world, and the moral and spiritual fears about what it means to literally act as gods, creators.

At the moment, though, the greatest danger is that we won't pay attention to this new way of being human, this incredible increase in our power as a species. To ignore this issue is to duck history.

—Bill McKibben
August 2003
author,
Enough: Staying Human in an Engineered Age
Reprinted and revised by permission from the Institute
for Agriculture and Trade Policy from their booklet,
The Ownership of Life:
When Patents and Values Crash by Martin Teitel and
Hope Shand

Introduction

Life Patents and Monopolies on Genes, Diseases, Plants, and Animals

The Greenberg children are worth hundreds of thousands of dollars.

Jonathan and Amy Greenberg both died from a rare neurological disorder called Canavan disease. The symptoms of Canavan disease appear in infants; children with the disease cannot crawl, walk, sit, or talk. Most children with the disease die before the age of 11.

While still infants, the Greenberg children became the basis for a national effort in 1981 to find the genetic causes of the disease. Jonathan and Amy's parents contacted other families affected with the disease and developed relationships with genetic researchers. More than 160 families contributed blood and tissue towards the research.

The collaborative effort paid off. In 1993, Dr. Reuben Matalon, a researcher at Miami Children's Hospital, discovered mutations on a specific gene that had some correlation to the disease. The discovery, as with all discoveries that claim a genetic cause for a disease, was a long way from an actual cure, but the families hoped it was a beginning.

In the meantime, Matalon developed a test that would screen for the mutations.

Unbeknownst to the families, Miami Children's Hospital applied for, and won, a patent on the gene. Using that patent, the hospital limited and even shut down other testing and research into Canavan disease. By claiming a monopoly over the genetic mutations of the Canavan disease, the hospital demanded royalties and limited the number of times the test was used. The hospital used the blood and tissue of Jonathan, Amy, and other children to find the genetic mutations, and then restricted research into the very disease that ended up taking their lives.

"What the hospital has done is a desecration of the good that has come from our children's short lives," Jonathan and Amy's father told *The Chicago Tribune*, "I can't look at it any other way."[1]

Judith Tsipis had a son who also died of Canavan: "We gave our DNA and that of our children to help develop testing and prenatal diagnosis. Is it right that they use our genes—given to help others—in a way that restricts access and increases cost to testing?"[2]

"This case is the ultimate nightmare of how a gene patent can be used against the very families who made possible the discovery of the gene," Tsipis said.[3] In November 2000, Tsipis and other families who had donated their DNA filed suit against the hospital. The families felt that their children's blood and tissue had not been used for the public good but for profit. The hospital stood to earn over $375,000 in royalties annually from the test.[4]

The Canavan disease gene patent is one of 20,000 life patents that have been granted by the U.S. Patent Office.[5] Another 25,000 are pending. The case is just one illustration of how the patent system is being used to halt important medical research and rob biological material from individuals and groups.

It is a legal right in the United States to take out patents on human genes, deadly diseases, whole animal species, plants, seeds, and foodstuffs. Critics call these patents "life patents." Life patents are the biotechnology and agrochemical industries' dirty little secret. Through these life patents, the patent system is being manipulated by universities, research institutions, and corporations to create monopolies over things that they haven't invented, over things that were "invented" by nature. Agrochemical companies have applied for hundreds of patents on rice and corn. U.S. corporations are patenting genes they have taken from Chinese villagers, the entire population of Iceland, and many other ethnic groups. Companies and universities now claim to have invented whole diseases, such as staph infection and tuberculosis. Thousands of patents have been awarded that cover human genes, human proteins, and other molecules found in the human body.

Patents have been historically associated with heroic inventors and entrepreneurs who create advances that improve our lifestyles. In our elementary school history books we read about the fame and honor that came with patents by Thomas Edison, Alexander Graham Bell, and Mary Dixon Kies, who, in 1809, became the first woman to be awarded a patent.[6] Their inventions, recognized by patents, changed the world and made the United States a more comfortable and healthy place to live.

Why, then, are patents now being used to slow scientific innovation, as was the case with the Canavan disease genes? Why are other life patents being used to monopolize plants and foodstuffs? Why do some critics, such as Vandana Shiva, director of the Research Foundation for Science, Technology, and Natural Resource Policy, call the granting of life patents "intellectual and cultural rape?"[7]

In July 2000, Todd Dickinson, the former director of the United States Patent and Trademark Office, sat before a Congressional subcommittee and explained why a particular form of life patent, patents on human genes, was necessary. The justification for allowing all life patents lies in his statement and the statements of the string of biotechnology executives and patent lawyers who followed him.

Life patents stimulate research, the pro-patent witnesses claimed. "Without the funding and incentives that are provided by the patent system," Dickinson said, "research into the basis of genetic diseases and the development of tools for the diagnosis and treatment of such diseases would be significantly curtailed."[8]

Why, then, would a group of families affected by Canavan disease be angry at a hospital that patented their children's biological make-up? If life patents are meant to spur innovation and hasten the search for medical cures, why wouldn't a group of parents support patents on "disease genes" that directly affect the lives of their children?

In Chapter One, we will see how, as in the Canavan disease gene case, life patents are demonstrably counterproductive in the fight against disease. Companies are now patenting the diseases themselves like tuberculosis and staph infection. Instead of helping to prevent or cure these diseases, however, the race for these patents engenders secrecy in research and creates walls between scientists. As well, in the war against "super bugs," a new breed of pathogens that are resistant to all antibiotics, life patents hinder the sharing of scientific data. Patents are also given on so-called "disease genes," human genes whose mutations correlate to certain health conditions. Again, the fight against the actual diseases is slowed because important human genes are monopolized by single institutions. The exciting new world of genetic research is being controlled not by the desire to learn more about the biology but by the desire for profits in the short term. By paralyzing medical research, life patents could be costing lives.

"The Patent System is one of the strongest bulwarks of democratic government today," states an educational pamphlet put out by the United States Patent and Trademark Office. "It offers the same protection, the same opportunity, the same hope of reward to every individual. For a hundred ninety one years it has recognized, as it will continue to recognize, the inherent right of an inventor to his government's protection. The American Patent System plays no favorites."

The pamphlet provides a noble view of the U.S. patent system, but many populations who have witnessed the consequences of life patents would not agree. The international pursuit for monopolies through life patents begins long before the laboratory and affects more than just the scientists. The biological resources—such as plants, natural medicines, and even human cell lines—of dozens of indigenous groups and developing countries are being patented by Western companies. Chapter Two will look at the "mining" of biological materials throughout the world in pursuit of life patents, enforceable through international treaties.[9] Representatives of these groups call this mining of biological resources "biocolonialism" or "biopiracy." They see the practice as anything but giving the "same protection, the same opportunity, the same hope of reward to every individual," as the Patent Office hopes. For many, the U.S. patent system does play favorites. Biotechnology and pharmaceutical companies reap the rewards of the patent system while those less powerful are exploited.

But don't life patents help bring biotechnology products to market? And aren't "products" of the biotechnology industry going to make this a better, more healthy world? What could serve the public good more than products and tools that will fight suffering and pain?

Universities, biotechnology firms, agrochemical companies, and the politicians that support them imply that, through biotechnology and genetic research, our lives will some day be free from disease. The rhetoric of the biotechnology industry often promises to uncover why we have cancer, why we are fat and bald, and why we are depressed. It promises us the arrival of super pills and genetically engineered happiness. In order to sell the $3 billion government genome project to Congress and the American public, the scientists advocating the project promised that "the best, perhaps only, way to alleviate disease was to map the entire genome."[10] Other scientists declare that the study of genetics will cure our psychological "defects." The rhetoric of the biotech industry promises to explain why bad things happen to good people and then the biotech industry says it will fix them.

The rhetoric has worked—and is repeated by politicians, the media, and our next-door neighbors—because it fits in rather well with society's hope in science and our own desire for a less painful world. As well, it sounds so good. Who wouldn't want to live in a world without disease? Science has done great things so far, why not this?

As we will see in Chapter Three, the rhetoric of the biotech industry offers promises that cannot be kept. Our genes do not hold the secrets to our health. Less than 10% of our diseases can be said to be genetically caused. The most common diseases that plague our society—cancer, heart disease, diabetes—are caused by a combination of genes, environment, and lifestyle. Seventy percent of stroke, colon cancer, coronary heart disease and type II diabetes could be prevented if patients changed their lifestyles.[11] More and more of our studies are proving that research into our lifestyles and our environment is a better battleground against disease than at the molecular level.

It is true that scientists need to know how our DNA reacts to and interacts with our environment in order to better understand diseases. But while the possibility of prevention lies in changing our environments and lifestyles, the biotechnology industry is concentrating only on the molecular level. The industry hopes to create cures—not prevention—for our diseases by manipulating or creating therapies for the genes alone. "Overly enthusiastic expectations regarding the benefits of genetic research for disease prevention have the potential to distort research priorities and spending for health," Harvard epidemiologist Walter C. Willett says. "The inherent problem is that most pharmacologic strategies do not address the underlying causes of ill health in Western countries which are not drug deficiencies... The use of research approaches that integrate environmental factors including diet and other life-style variables with genetic information has the potential to clarify the roles of both environment and genotype in disease causation."[12]

The integrated studies that Willett hopes for have little chance of surviving the restrictions of life patents (and the lawsuits that inevitably follow them). Instead, the biotechnology industry has settled for a particular product from life patents—genetic tests. Genetic tests may make a few biotechnology companies money now, but do little to prevent or cure disease in the long term.

Genetic tests are, at best, questionable both in their accuracy and their usefulness to patients. In fact, these tests have proven to have a disastrous impact on society and human health. Lives and ethics have been sacrificed in the race for quick-fix biotech products.

Chapter Four will look at the American patent system in more detail. In particular, the Patent Office's requirements for an "invention" and the winding road through the courts that life patents have taken. Many of us can understand how one might patent a mousetrap. If it is constructed in a way that has never been tried before and demonstrates an innovative new way to catch mice, then the inventor should be rewarded with an exclusive right to market and sell that mousetrap, at least for a while. But how is it possible that those same patent rules apply to a mouse? How can one claim to have invented an animal? Or a plant? Or human DNA? Shouldn't mice be treated differently from mousetraps? One striking point comes across clearly: According to the patent system's own broad definition of an invention, they should be.

Proponents further claim that patents have been essential elements in previous booms in U.S. technology. Therefore, patents on genes, plants, and animals are essential to the success of the biotechnology industry. "We stand in the midst of an information revolution that rivals the great renaissances of centuries past," Dickinson told the Congressional subcommittee.

"Just as the patent system has nurtured the development of telephony, aeronautics, and computers, so, too, will it ensure that the new discoveries in genomics lead to healthier, longer lives for all of humankind."[13]

It is ironic that Dickinson used the example of aeronautics as a technological industry in which patents were essential. Instead of being promoted through stringent patent laws, the early success of the aeronautical industry was more dependent on the *loosening* of patent protection, as we will see in Chapter Five. It cannot be denied there is a real fear within the biotech industry that, if life patents are taken away, the industry will lose investors, the U.S. will fall behind in medical technologies, and, ultimately, the national economy may suffer. But these are questionable assumptions at best. Chapter Five demonstrates how life patents, contrary to what is often claimed, are paralyzing the development of the biotechnology industry and threaten the U.S. economy at large. Like the dot.com industry, the fortune that has been made in biotechnology has been generated by investors and stocks, not from the sale of real products to real customers. Further, the future of biotechnology is in danger of going the way of the dot.coms unless the industry ceases using life patents that tie up basic research. For the biotechnology industry, real profits are still pending.

A final claim by proponents of life patents is that such patents are guaranteed by the Constitution. Randal Scott, President of Incyte Genomics, told the Congressional subcommittee: "Given the impact of genomic inventions on health care, the award of patents on these inventions is entirely consistent with the Constitution's goal of granting patents to enable "progress in science and the useful arts."[14]

Chapter Six shows the distance between the original intentions of the patent as embodied in the Constitution and the way it is used on pieces of biology today. The United States Patent and Trademark Office was set up to reward inventors while assuring that inventions would be used for the public good. Through the forethought of the writers of the Constitution, the patent system was set up to protect basic property rights. By publishing the protected invention, it was thought that further innovations would be spurred.

In this history we see the prescient clarity of the Patent Office's first director, Thomas Jefferson. Long before life patents were even conceived, Jefferson worried about how one might manipulate the patent system to develop harmful monopolies. Jefferson, and others with him, questioned whether scientific ideas should be allowed to be patented at all. With U.S. patents now being used worldwide to monopolize food sources and exploit both individuals and whole cultures, Jefferson's greatest fears have come to pass.

We have only to turn to those directly affected by life patents to ponder some of the ethical questions that underlie these issues. The Greenberg family and other families affected by Canavan disease ask: What right do companies have to do what they want with our bodies and gain a profit from our pain? Farmers of indigenous foods ask: Hasn't society progressed beyond "colonization ethics," the idea that an entity can own a piece of something or somebody simply because the entity is more powerful, more wealthy, or employs more lawyers? We, the taxpayers of the United States might ask: How is it that our taxpayers' money is being used to support medical research that is kept secret from other scientists?

How do we confront the monopolies that life patents engender? Must we, like the British poet Donna MacLean, all walk into the patent office and apply for a patent on our own bodies in order to stop corporations from doing the same?[15] Or, like Jeremy Rifkin and Stuart Newman, do we need to start submitting patents for a broad range of possible future scenarios—in their case every possible mammal-human combination of cells—just to keep research institutions from doing the same?[16]

We cannot completely fault the Patent Office. With thousands of life patent applications waiting to be decided upon, some as long as 400,000 pages, the USPT itself can be considered a bureaucratic victim of the race for life patents.[17] The question is whether the 190 PhD employees working for the Patent Office's biotech department should be put in charge of awarding ownership over plants, animals, and human genes.

This book does not promise to answer these questions. What it does do is propose that the issue of life patents needs examining, and not just by the Patent Office or industry lawyers and biotechnology scientists. This book will demonstrate that life patents do not help our economy, they are a hindrance to scientific research, and, ultimately, an obstacle to fighting the diseases which plague society. Further, life patents are not protected by the Constitution, they are simply what we have ended up with after two decades of legal acumen from the biotechnology industry. Instead of simply accepting this situation, the country as a whole needs to decide if it wants to allow life patents.

Some say that politics should be kept out of science. Public and legislative discussions on the exploration of the natural world will only slow down progress, this argument goes, and science will become a victim to the whims of politicians and ideological debates. But the search for knowledge about the natural world does not occur in a vacuum. Scientific experiments and observations in this country now occur in the context of universities that want to attract funding, multinational corporations that want to please their investors, and governmental institutions that struggle with bureaucracies. The desired end of nearly any research in genetics is not simply to learn more about the human body or to find a cure for diseases. Biotechnology companies are under pressure to develop products from the knowledge. Universities want to attract students and funding. Government research institutions need to prove they are worthy of taxpayer's money. In other words, scientific experiments are already political. They are influenced and driven by many more factors than simply the pursuit of knowledge.

As will be demonstrated within the context of life patents, scientific research has a tremendous effect and is tremendously affected by business, the economy, law, international relations, social and cultural norms, and government policy. Genetic science is more than just a group of scientists studying chemicals because they want to learn more about the human body. Their experiments affect not only our society but also the world at large.

Research and technology—and the patents that protect or hinder them—are key areas of political and public concern. If politics means the democratic debate of where our country is headed now and in the future, then, yes, politics should be very involved in science. As was true in Thomas Jefferson's era, technology is deeply political. So too are patents.

Genetic research presents a potentially promising future for learning more about our bodies and our natural world. Ultimately, it may have some positive effects on medicine and public health. The policy of allowing patents on life, however, threatens that future. The goal of a select few who own and control life is a positive annual report, not the progress of science and medicine. By eliminating the policy of granting patents on life, we have the opportunity to take back our future. Perhaps we can even change the future for children like Jonathan and Amy Greenberg.

CHAPTER ONE

Buy, Sell, Sue

How Life Patents Kill Innovation

> The right to search for truth implies also a duty: one must not conceal any part of what one has recognized to be true.
>
> –Albert Einstein, inscribed
> on his statue in front of the
> National Academy of
> Sciences[1]

In 1990, geneticist Mary-Claire King finally found what she had spent nearly fifteen years in her laboratory searching for—a correlation between breast cancer and a tract of DNA on chromosome 17. King's research pointed to the general location of what would become known as the "breast cancer gene" or, as King herself dubbed it, BRCA1.[2]

Both government and private researchers throughout the world took immediate interest. Breast cancer affects one in eight women in the United States. Each year, 180,000 new cases are reported. Throughout the United States and Europe, researchers wanted to be the first to find the exact location of BRCA1, both in the hope for more knowledge about the disease and for the immense commercial market that any cure or therapy promised.

The race for the gene was facilitated by a public database called the Breast Cancer Linkage Consortium (BCLC) which freely shared the work of King and other researchers with both public and private groups.[3] Dr. Francis Collins, a noted geneticist who would later head the government's genome project, was excited by King's work. He convinced King to collaborate with his team at the National Institutes of Health (NIH) on the search for BRCA1.

Then, in 1994, the promising search for BRCA1 ground to an abrupt halt. The four-year King and Collins collaboration disintegrated. King was reportedly devastated and disillusioned.[4] The reason: Myriad Genetics, an upstart biotechnology firm based in Salt Lake City, had applied for a patent on the BRCA1 gene. The Myriad team had found the exact location of the gene—using the information published by the BCLC.

In a news conference soon after, however, King was optimistic, despite the fact that Myriad would soon hold a patent that was built on nearly 20 years of her research and the work of many others. She spoke of the hope that would be given to women by the future exploration of BRCA1. "In the 20 years since we have been working on this project, more than a million women have died of breast cancer," King said. "We very much hope that something we do in the next 20 years will preclude another million women dying of the disease."[5]

Supporters of life patents often quote Abraham Lincoln's line: "Patents are the fuel on the fire of genius." According to this idea, research on BRCA1 should have been greatly stimulated after the patent was awarded. A private company whose "property" was now protected by a patent would theoretically use its best resources to search for a cure for breast cancer. Indeed, most researchers agree that the private sector was once the best place to develop the products derived from genetic research, including cures, therapies, and drugs.

In fact, we have not seen Lincoln's "fuel on the fire of genius," much less a little lighter fluid, promised for the study on the BRCA1 gene. Myriad indeed produced a product, but it was not a cure for breast cancer. Myriad developed a test that screened individuals for the gene mutations.

And that was that. No invigorated research for a cure that King had hoped for. Her twenty years of research gave a company a test that, when looked at closely (as we do in Chapter five), does little more than confirm risk factors that were commonly known before the gene was discovered.

As Dr. Donald Bruce, director of the Society, Religion, and Technology Project, put it: "Years of patient research by several groups got close to locating the first gene [for breast cancer], but at the last minute a newly set-up US company hustled in, did the last few steps and claimed the whole gold seam as their own private property."[6]

Myriad has since been given at least eight other patents on a number of so-called BRCA genes, including the second "breast cancer gene" dubbed BRCA2. Basically Myriad has patents that cover all the BRCA genes and all the ways of looking at the genes.

What is Myriad doing with its monopoly over the BRCA genes? The company has a $4 million strategic alliance with Eli Lilly pharmaceutical company that is "focused on addressing the therapeutic potential of the BRCA1 gene," according to a press release by the company.[7] But the research partnership with Eli Lilly is by far the least funded of all Myriad's $447 million worth of collaborations.[8] Instead, Myriad's resources appear to be directed toward replicating what they did with its patents on BRCA—finding and exploiting the next "gold seam" of DNA.

The BRCA patents are in the hands of one company that, having invested little, now has a profitable genetic test that it can market. As might have been expected, the year Myriad was awarded the patent the company showed a $1.5 million increase in genetic testing revenues.[9] "Once testing becomes routine, which we still expect eventually," *Biotechnology Quarterly* reported in 1998, "BRACAnalysis [the commercial name of the BRCA genetic tests] would tap a $150-200 million U.S. market."[10]

Patenting a "tract" of DNA means that anyone else who discovers something within that tract must then work through the company or university that owns it, often involving teams of lawyers, agreements, contracts, and royalty payments. The entity that owns the patent may have little idea what is in the tract, and may have no intention of exploring it, but it knows that it can demand payment for anything discovered within it.

After Myriad was awarded the BRCA1 patent, the company sent a letter to the University of Pennsylvania demanding that they pay every time the university used the BRCA1 genetic test. The university's Genetics Diagnostics Laboratory had been conducting BRCA1 gene screening as part of a study sponsored by the National Cancer Institute (NCI).[11] "In reality, this lab has been stopped from testing for BRCA1 and BRCA2," Arupa Ganguly, research and development director of the university's laboratory, said.[12]

"It seems that in this country, if you have a patent, that's it, you can monopolize testing," Ganguly told *The Scientist*. "It's outrageous... This will happen with every gene that can be patented."[13]

Myriad contacted laboratories worldwide demanding sole right to perform the test. The company has even gone so far as to request that all BRCA tests be performed at its own laboratories in Salt Lake City. A number of non-profit European laboratories reacted with disgust. "We do not want to support this patent," Bernhard Weber, who uses a similar test in a German laboratory, told *Nature*. "We need to get our results based on our own technology."[14]

Otmar Kloiber, senior executive of the German Medical Association, went to the heart of the matter: "The substance patents now being given to the human genome are inappropriate and endanger research and medicine. Information about the human genome can't be invented. It is the common heritage of all humans."[15]

In the quest for profit through patents, genetic research is losing (or has lost) an element that science has long held sacred: the shared ownership and free exchange of research results and approaches.[16] This chapter will look at how life patents have restricted or halted scientific progress, taken essential research tools away from scientists and doctors, and allowed super infections to get the upper hand in human health.

Life patents hinder American innovation and inventiveness—but the science of genetics is not in the same category as computers or cell phone technology. Genetics involves scientific advancements that could improve human health where hindered innovation translates into loss of human lives. The health of individuals and public health as a whole lose when knowledge is kept secret or tied up in exclusive contracts. Although the majority of genetic research is funded with taxpayers' money, taxpayer's health is being ignored.

In later chapters, we'll look at patents that cover animals, plants, and molecules that have been bioengineered. In these patents, the claimed invention is not something found "naturally," but a molecule or living thing in which the molecular chemistry has been changed or added to. There is an important argument to be made against allowing these bioengineered life forms to be patented but we will address that later. In this chapter, a different type of life patent is examined: patents on genomes or on specific genes of living things *as they are found in nature or in our bodies*.

Patenting Killer Diseases

> The debate over access to DNA sequence data is raging among researchers studying species from viruses to Homo Sapiens. But it is especially heated when it comes to the sequencing of pathogens, where holding back data, even for a year or less, arguably could cost human lives. Yet in this area, withholding sequence data is commonplace.
>
> –Eliot Marshall in *Science*[17]

"We are committed to an arms race," Dr. Bruce Levin told visitors from Britain's House of Lords in 1997.[18] Levin is not a professor of military or political science. He and his colleagues research population biology at Emory University. And Levin's "arms race" is not against terrorists or missile-laden enemies. Levin's arms race is against infectious diseases, the world's number one cause of death.

Fifty years ago, scientists were sure they had won this war. With the development of penicillin and other antibiotics in the 1950s, medical experts declared that infectious diseases would soon be an antiquated chapter in our history books. Doctor and writer Lewis Thomas describes the optimistic years of his internship when antibiotics were first being introduced:

> For an intern, it was the opening of a whole new world. We had been raised to be ready for one kind of profession, and we sensed that the profession itself had changed at the moment of our entry. We know that other molecular variations of sulfanilamide were on their way from industry, and we heard about the possibility of penicillin and other antibiotics; we became convinced, overnight, that nothing lay beyond reach for the future.[19]

Instead, the diseases not only survived, but some evolved into super bugs that became more and more resistant to all drugs. Multi-drug resistant tuberculosis strains (MDR-TB), or "Ebola with wings," as they have been called, top this list.

The U.S. Centers for Disease Control ranks the threat of these drug-resistant bugs on the same level as biological warfare and uses the same military terms to talk about the enemy: "Infectious diseases increasingly threaten public health and contribute significantly to the escalating costs of health care," it stated in its performance plans for 1999 and 2000. "They are a continuing menace to all segments of society, regardless of age, gender, lifestyle, ethnic background and socioeconomic status."[20]

Many of these drug-resistant super bugs are evolving not from exotic diseases but from some of our most common ailments. The most common source of fatal infections in hospitals, staphylococcus, is a prime example. In 1995, 13,550 patients in New York City hospitals alone contracted the infection, resulting in 1,400 deaths and costing $435 million.[21] Now we face its evolved counterpart, a particularly nasty infection called *vancomycin intermediate resistant Staphylococcus aureus* (VISA). Doctors found antibiotics useless against VISA when it nearly killed a baby in Japan in 1996 and two other patients in the U.S. the next year.

And the enemy continues to beef up its battlefront. Researchers recently discovered how the staph infection overcomes the defenses of the body's immune system and the drugs we use to help it. The bugs "simply swap DNA with their relatives to acquire the genes needed to overcome it," stated a press release by the National Institute of Allergy and Infectious Diseases. "And they do so quite readily."[22]

Researchers in Japan found that the staph bug evolves at an amazing rate and can overcome new drugs within months. Keiichi Hiramatsu, a scientist at Juntendo University, points out that a new antibiotic called Methicillin has already been beaten by an evolved staph bug. The super bug appeared on the scene just one year after Methicillin was launched. Hiramatsu's team also found staph was "capable of generating numerous new toxins and assaulting human bodies." These new toxins could spark uncontrollable immune reactions in people.[23]

If humans lost this war against the super bugs and antibiotics were rendered useless, then transplants, chemotherapy and many other more common medical procedures we take for granted would become impossible. Health care for all of us would revert to levels that predate the 1940s.

Biotechnology could hold one of the keys to solving this threat. Scientists have completely sequenced the genomes— mapped out the DNA found in the chromosome of a cell—of at least 13 pathogens and another 28 are in the works. By studying these disease genomes, scientists may be able to find vaccines or drugs necessary to battle the super bugs. At the very least, scientists should be able to learn more about the enemy. Scientists may even be able to find a way to keep the pathogens from getting to us in the first place.

A wealth of resources is available to fight these public health battles. The U.S. has the greatest medical research facilities and scientists in the world. According to advocates of life patents, intellectual property rights are designed to help us win just these kind of wars because they stimulate investment and give incentive for scientific breakthroughs. Advocates of life patents, like the president of Incyte Genomics Randal W. Scott, claim that scientists, protected by patent rights, will search diligently for new medical technologies: "Existing patent guidelines, which have spurred the tremendous advances we've recently seen in medical research, must remain intact to ensure continued discovery," he told a Congressional subcommittee.[24] Through the patent system, industry, government, and academia should be able to work together to beat the super bugs.

The patent system, however, may force us to lose this war. Winning this battle requires cooperation among scientists with a free flow of information. But as corporations patent the genomes of these super bugs, their tendency has been to withhold vital information from other researchers and the government is forced to spend millions of dollars duplicating their research.

Staph infection is a prime example. In the mid 1990s, microbiologist John Iandolo gave a biotech company called Human Genome Sciences (HGS) the DNA it needed to decode the staph genome.[25] HGS made some progress on its research but then refused to share information with others unless they agreed that all intellectual property rights remain with the company. No scientist agreed to such stringent terms. In the meantime, HGS garnered $9 million for research on staph from the drug company Pharmacia & Upjohn.[26]

Iandolo, now a professor of microbiology and immunology

at the University of Oklahoma, told the *Los Angeles Times*: "I feel that industry doesn't care as much about [public health] scares as they do about making a buck."

"When it became clear they were not going to share this," Iandolo said, "we decided to get into the genome business ourselves and make it clear we would share it with everyone." Iandolo moved to government-funded research of staph at the University of Oklahoma.[27]

At least two other biotechnology companies have deciphered the staph genome but they too have been unwilling to freely share their research. Genome Therapeutics Corp. (GTC) has a $44 million partnership with Schering-Plough on the staph genome[28] and Incyte Pharmaceuticals sells its staph data to a whole series of other pharmaceutical companies.[29]

Private companies have a long history of sharing basic research on diseases, so government officials and scientists were completely taken by surprise by the corporations' unwillingness to share data on staph. The biotech and pharmaceutical companies had always been interested in patenting drugs that would fight diseases. But with the bug so clearly a dangerous threat to public health, government scientists never suspected that industry would try owning the actual disease itself.

"Without this information, we don't have the insights we need," says John La Montagne, deputy director of the National Institute of Allergy and Infectious Diseases. "It's like keeping the map of the city of Washington secret."[30]

As a major public health threat, however, the government had to put up some kind of fight against staph. Subsequently, publicly funded projects deciphering the staph genome got off to a late start and had to begin from scratch. Staph investigators, like Dr. Olaf Schneewind of UCLA, estimated in a *Los Angeles Times* article that the setback slowed research by four or five years and cost the U.S. taxpayer millions of dollars.

"From the perspective of industry, you can view this as a market," Schneewind said. "At the same time, there is a humanitarian issue."[31]

"At the end of the road is a product that will benefit the public," Francis Collins, director of the government's Genome Project, said about the pathogen patents. "All this secrecy being applied is putting a lot of toll booths on that road."[32]

It's an all too apt analogy. These tollbooths cost money—$17 million a year for the government to study disease-causing bugs. Like their counterparts on the highway, they slow things down and waste time. And in this race, time is critical.

Damming Up Science

When companies and universities keep information on these super bugs secret, it is like having generals in a war who don't talk to each other. We thought we had beat tuberculosis, one of the most destructive bugs of all, fifty years ago. Instead, researchers estimate that 3.5 million people are now dying of tuberculosis, an increase of nearly 40% since 1990.[33] Nearly 1% of the world's population is newly infected every year and by the year 2020, 1,000 million people will be infected.[34] As of 1999, the Committee on the Elimination of Tuberculosis under the Institute of Medicine reported that 58 different private companies or industry-affiliated academic groups were working on diagnostic tools for tuberculosis. According to the committee's report, sixteen of those companies refused to discuss "even the format of the tools in development or the target matrix." The majority of the remaining firms appeared to be duplicating each other's research, leading the committee to conclude "there are many fewer diagnostic approaches than there are industry or academic test developers." At the same time, the committee observed a "dramatic increase in the numbers of tuberculosis-related patents issued over time."[35]

"Tuberculosis, like Staph aureus and H. pylori will be sequenced many times over in part because sequencers aren't sharing data, whether for business reasons or because of interlab rivalries,"[36] *Science* writer Eliot Marshall reported in 1997.

Marshall found that staph and tuberculosis are not the only diseases that companies can now own, buy, and sell through the patent process. In 1995, GTC sequenced and subsequently sold the genome of the bacterium that causes ulcers, called Helicobacter pylori, for $22 million.[37] Data concerning the H. pylori bacteria is now in the hands of a Swedish drug company who charges a fee for access. The company does not plan on making the information public. Applications have also been filed that will give patents over pathogens that are responsible for meningitis, ulcers, and pneumonia.[38]

The most recent race to patent a disease occurred in the spring of 2003 when a mysterious and quick-spreading disease named severe acute respiratory syndrome, or SARS, emerged in Asia. Within a few weeks of the discovery of SARS, several biotechnology companies had already applied for patents on the genome of the virus.

"It's very competitive, but we think we are the early bird," Hailson Yu at the University of Hong Kong said. The university claimed it had begun negotiations with commercial companies as early as May 2003 for a diagnostic test which would stem from the desired SARS patent.[39]

If a patent is awarded on the SARS genome or on its genes, the owner would be able to control who researched the disease and all commercial profit from vaccines or cures would go to the patent holder. Scientists are unsure exactly what other entities have applied for the patent—and unsure who has the most up to date genetic information on the disease—since the Patent Office does not publish prospective patents.

Donald Low, chief microbiologist at Mount Sinai Hospital, saw the race for the SARS patent as a bad start to fighting the disease: "There are those looking at this from the vantage point of making money... just looking at opportunities."[40]

Patenting genes such as BRCA and actual diseases such as SARS gives one entity control of what scientists sometimes call "upstream knowledge." Comparing scientific knowledge to a stream is a useful metaphor. If you claim ownership of water close to its source—say, if you dam a stream high in the mountains—then you have the power to either monopolize all that water for your own use or control how the water will be used downstream. Knowledge works the same way. Like water, it is most useful when it is freely shared at the downstream level. It is at this downstream level that scientists take basic science and turn it into useful technologies. Patents on genes and genomes, like the water dam, allow monopolies on basic science. Meanwhile scientists working on downstream uses for the knowledge—turning the knowledge into cures or finding whole new ways of looking at the molecular material—are cut off from the knowledge or must pay for its use.

Inherent in the complex enterprise of science is the need for scientists to test each others findings and data. Sharing upstream knowledge is critical to verifying what has been found or created, and to uncover flaws and errors. In essence, this is the nature of scientific discovery and the search for scientific "truths:" hypothesize, experiment, test, and retest.

When scientists keep their research on pathogens secret, their data cannot be checked or explored by other scientists. Without the benefit of shared research, scientists will not know the pathogens as well as they should. Sequencing and identifying super bugs by fast computers is different from knowing how they work. It is like knowing the color of an enemy army's uniform, but not knowing what kind of weapons they carry.

Further, if you dam upstream knowledge with patents, then it will be more difficult to find the causes of diseases or to produce downstream products. In the case of biotechnology, downstream products theoretically will be therapeutic drugs or vaccines that come from research on upstream knowledge, though we have yet to see these. Downstream products such as these, rightly perhaps, should be patented and owned, at least for a while. But by patenting the disease itself, by granting ownership of the problem, it becomes much more difficult to find preventions or cures for those problems.

Summarizing the research into pathogen genomes, molecular geneticist George M. Weinstock notes that, in contrast to private genome projects, "a near universal trend among public (but not private) genome projects is the early release of unfinished sequence data... The availability of this sequence data not only generates hypotheses but also greatly speeds the task of testing them."[41] Simply sequencing these pathogens but then not comparing research results leaves us with little understanding of the diseases themselves, Weinstock explained in an October 2000 article in the journal *Emerging Infectious Diseases*. In order to understand these pathogens, Weinstock suggests that the results of different groups of researchers need to be compared to one another. Strains of the same pathogens may behave differently or a given pathogen may have different effects on different kinds of tissue. Our knowledge of these pathogens will be less than it should be if the research results on each of these strains is not shared and medicines developed in isolation from related research will not be as effective as they could be.

Somewhat deflated, Weinstock ends his article with a prediction: "In any event, it is likely that candidate genes will be identified and enter industrial development long before researchers understand their role in infection."[42] Unless researchers share their discoveries about the enemy, the efficacy of our weapons against the super bugs will be suspect.

"We'll Tell You About It After the Patent"

This problem of secrecy goes beyond pathogens and is rampant throughout genetic research. A 1997 survey conducted by Dr. David Blumenthal of Massachusetts General Hospital found that genetic researchers restrict free exchange of research results more than all other life science researchers. His study, published in *The Journal of the American Medical Association*, found that 34% of the 2167 life science researchers surveyed had been denied access to research results from other institutions.[43] When compared with others studying life science, it was found that geneticists in particular kept more results secret. "The precise reasons for geneticists' greater proclivity to withhold data should be the subject of future research," Blumenthal noted. One of the reasons, the report theorized, was that withholding of results was a sort of cultural norm, a "prevailing attitude," within the genetics field.

The survey's findings imply that this cultural norm and prevailing attitude within genetics was created by the race for patents:

> Involvement in commercialization and participation in AIRRs [academic-industry research relationships] are significantly associated with the tendency of life science faculty to withhold the results of their research.

Nearly twenty percent of all life science researchers surveyed reported delaying the release of their own research results by more than six months in the past three years. The main reason given was the need to wait for a patent application.

Five years later, a similar study shows that withholding results of research in genetics is only getting worse. A 2002 survey found that 47% of university geneticists had been denied access to other scientists' research results. Because of that, some reported that they could not confirm the validity of experiments conducted by other scientists because the results were not being fully disclosed.[44] Theories and hypothesis by geneticists are not being tested and confirmed by their peers. In essence, the attitude of withholding data is eroding the scientific method in genetic research.

"At one time, if you found something exciting, you would run down the corridor and talk about it," biologist Derry Roopenian at Jackson Laboratory told *Scientific American*.

"Now, if you discover something but a commercial backer is interested in it, you can't say a word about it."[45]

Other studies have shown that life science researchers working under sponsorship of private companies typically refrain from publishing results for more than six months.[46] The National Institutes of Health (NIH) suggest that two months should be the maximum waiting period before releasing results. Why withhold your results for more than six months? Wouldn't a scientist be excited to broadcast the success of new research? The studies show that companies or universities sponsoring the research are much more interested in claiming patents than they are interested in kudos from their peers. They delay publication of research results in order to have time to apply for a patent.

The words "research results" are cold, utilitarian terms. The phrase "six months before releasing results" means very little until one places human lives on every one of the 180 days that make up six months.

"External pressures on scientists, such as evaluations for academic promotion and the need to secure funding, increase the tendency to view competition as against other scientists rather than against the disease," Steven A. Rosenberg, chief of surgery at the National Cancer Institute, wrote in a now famous letter to *The New England Journal of Medicine*.[47] Later he commented, "It is a very clear moral issue. If you withhold information, you potentially delay progress. If you delay progress, you potentially delay the development of effective treatments, and human beings suffer and die who need not have done so."[48]

Owning a Gene You Know Nothing About

It's like patenting an airplane that doesn't have a tail. They know it won't fly, but they'll stop everyone who has an airplane with a tail.

—John P. Moore, Aaron Diamond AIDS
Research Center, commenting on the CCR5
Patent by Human Genome Sciences[49]

In 1996, five groups of scientists almost simultaneously announced that they had found a human gene that played an important role in the deadly HIV/AIDS infection. This gene apparently codes for a receptor or docking site, called CCR5, that HIV uses to gain entry to a cell. The announcement was based on years of publicly-funded research that had been conducted by the NIH.[50] The discovery was heralded by AIDS activists and scientists alike as the first step toward developing a cellular "block" against AIDS. By 2000, 36 million people worldwide had been infected with the AIDS virus, 1.2 million of whom were children.[51]

But a Maryland biotech company called Human Genome Sciences (HGS) already claimed ownership of the CCR5 cell surface receptor in a patent it had applied for a year earlier. Amazingly, the scientists at the company had no idea that CCR5 had any connection to AIDS at the time of their patent application. In fact, the gene was among hundreds that HGS had applied for while the company did mass sequencing of the human genome. In February 2000, the Patent Office granted HGS the patent on CCR5.

Now, all research and any possible new drugs that might be developed to block the HIV virus' entry into the cell will be controlled by one corporation. "If someone uses this gene in a drug discovery program… and does it for commercial purposes, they have infringed the patent," William Haseltine, Chairman and CEO of HGS told the *Los Angeles Times*.[52] "We'd be entitled not just to damages, but to double and triple damages." Within eight months of the patent announcement, HGS's stock shot up 111%.[53]

"As a society, we have to ask if [the CCR5 patent] is fair," Robert Gallo told *Science*. Gallo was a part of the team at the Institute of Human Virology at the University of Maryland that played a key role in identifying the receptor. He felt that the prize went to a company that had done simple DNA sequencing but had completely skipped the hard work of actually studying the function of the gene.[54] "If the patent office awards a patent to someone who clones a gene, even though they have no notion of its function and no real idea of its use, that would be like saying, 'I found a fungus, therefore I should get credit for penicillin,'" Gallo said.[55]

The NIH's National Advisory Council for Human Genome Research doubted the fairness of the patent as well. In a letter to the Commissioner of Patents and Trademarks the council wrote:

> Based on sequence similarity, a patent was granted on a new gene [CCR5] that was claimed to be a putative chemokine receptor. No evidence was given to define the ligand or for any biological role for the putative receptor, but broad claims about the utility of the receptor were allowed. The allowed patent included a statement that CCR5 could be a receptor for a virus (a claim that could be made for any cell surface molecule). Independent of knowledge of the filing of the patent, other investigators established that CCR5 is the key co-receptor for HIV, making CCR5 a very important potential drug target. The patent taught nothing that contributed to these later important discoveries, but now the holders can dominate the field. Moreover, this broad allowance makes no concession to the discoveres of the key piece of intellectual property, namely that CCR5 is an HIV co-receptor. Allowing broad, poorly substantiated claims creates, de facto, an unacceptable monopoly on all fields in which the new gene might be found to be of use.[56]

HGS Chairman Haseltine summed it up best: "The patent office does not reward perspiration. They reward priority. They don't care if someone spent 20 years to find an invention or 20 minutes."[57]

Not only did HGS not know the function of CCR5, the company also mapped it incorrectly in the first place. Soon after the patent office awarded HGS the CCR5 patent, serious mis-

takes were found in the original patent application.[58] In its rush
to stake a claim, HGS incorrectly identified a number of the
amino acids that make up the protein the gene codes for.
Nevertheless, unless it is challenged in court, HGS retains the
patent.

Virologist Christopher Broder, part of the NIH team that
made the CCR5 connection to HIV, was flabbergasted. He
accused the patent office of rewarding "armchair" research.[59]
"This is a perfect example of the rush to sequence [human
DNA]," Broder said. "They get it wrong. They don't know the
function. That is what I have problems with: the whole notion
of the rush to patent genes."[60]

"Patent protection of entire genomes of organisms could
have a devastating untoward impact on biomedical research,"
the National Advisory Council for Human Genome Research
wrote in its letter to the Patent Office. "Genome patents would
provide an unacceptable monopoly that neither teaches nor
enables discoveries that would promote human health and well-
being."[61]

Currently, HGS has been awarded patents on 162 human
gene uses. It has applications pending on over 7,500 more.[62]

And HGS is not alone. The top gene-patent holders—
Incyte Genomics, Celera Genomics, Hyseq, Millennium, and
HGS—have been awarded nearly 1,000 life patents among
them, and have applied for some 25,000 more.[63] Considering
that the human being has only about 32,000 genes, that's a lot
of upstream territory being grabbed up.

In fact, many observers have described the race to patent
genes as similar to the race to stake a claim during the gold rush
in the 19th century American West. The prospector often knew
little about the tract of land he claimed; he certainly wasn't sure
there would be gold. Nevertheless, he got there first by whatever method—the fastest horse, for one—and so won the rights to
search for his prize. In the words of HGS's Haseltine about his
company's CCR5 patent, gene prospectors similarly "are

rewarded for speculation."[64] Gene prospectors too are claiming "tracts" of the human body, literally maps of our genes, hoping that someday their "gold" will show up.

"These guys are the robber barons of the genetic age," observed Gregg Gonsalves about the CCR5 patent. Gonsalves is with the Treatment Action Group, a New York-based organization that lobbies for AIDS research. "They are going to patent everything they can get their hands on and squeeze as much money out of it they can."[65]

Ultimately, the gold prospecting analogy falls short. While gold prospectors claimed land where they thought seams of gold might be, they were never allowed to patent gold itself. No one has ever been allowed to patent a particular metal found in nature and then control all of its present and future functions and utilities. Yet we are allowing these types of monopolies on genes. CCR5 is a particular molecule found in the body that is now controlled by one company. All of its yet unknown functions and utilities, even if discovered years from now, will be under constant threat of lawsuit by that one company.

Owning a Gene That You Know a Little About

If it seems silly to allow patents on genes that we know so little about, what about genes that scientists have spent years studying and do know more about? In this case, it is even more important that such basic upstream knowledge be shared.

With some life patents, scientists not only have mapped biological material, they also claim to know that a specific DNA sequence affects the body's condition. For instance, in so-called "disease genes," scientists have found correlations between a specific DNA sequence and a particular disease or behavior. After decades of study, disease genes have been discovered that have some correlation to breast cancer, as we have seen, but also to Alzheimer's, cystic fibrosis, colon cancer, and leukemia. These are the genes that often appear in our newspaper headlines.

Disease genes make the news because, unlike the swaths of genes that have simply been mapped, the discovery of disease genes and their functions are the closest scientists have come to the promise that genetics may someday provide clues for preventing or curing certain diseases. Often buried in the news story about any particular disease gene, however, is the announcement that the company or university studying the gene has or will soon have a patent on it.

When a company or university applies for a patent on a disease gene, most often it claims that it wants to patent the gene because of the gene's diagnostic use. That diagnostic use is in the form of a genetic screening test. Genetic tests basically look at a cell from a given piece of tissue or blood, isolate the gene in question, and screen for mutations. Although much more complex than a pregnancy test, genetic tests act the same way in that they make certain claims about biological status by examining the body's chemicals. A patent on a disease gene, therefore, also gives ownership of the genetic test for that gene.

Because we still know so little about how our unique genetic make-up interacts with our environment and lifestyle, genetic tests are of questionable usefulness to individual patients. We'll see why in Chapter Three. However, genetic tests can be a key tool in learning how "disease genes" function and interact in different environments and with diverse lifestyles. Genetic tests are most useful in what are called epidemiological studies, research which looks at large groups of people and the prevalence and incidence of a disease within that group. Epidemiological studies—and the comparing and contrasting of research results from such studies—assist in creating the upstream knowledge necessary to come up with prevention, vaccines, or cures.

When a company or university patents a disease gene, research—both epidemiological and on individual patients—can only be done by the one entity who owns the gene or the company that has contracted with the patentee. "So-called disease gene patents claim the observation of an individual's genetic makeup at a disease-associated locus when done for the purpose of diagnosis," Jon F. Merz, from the Center for Bioethics at the University of Pennsylvania, writes. "They cover all methods of "looking at" that locus when done for the purpose of diagnosis, based on the basic discovery of a statistical association between genetic variability and disease or risk of disease."[66]

As in the case of Myriad's breast cancer gene test, many of those that own the patents to disease genes are more concerned with selling genetic tests to individual consumers than using the test hand in hand with epidemiological studies. By patenting a disease gene, and monopolizing the test that screens for it, the companies and universities stop real scientific research in order to gleam some profit off of a test that is of questionable utility and sometimes dubious accuracy for individual patients.

Disease genes, like the swaths of DNA that we know little about, are quickly being gobbled up in patents. During his research, Merz found that there are more than 40 broad disease gene patents. In a recent survey of 27 such "disease gene" patents, 14 were exclusively licensed.[67] That is, in more than half of the cases, patent owners restricted research on the disease gene to just one institution. Patent monopolies on disease genes are especially destructive to medical science. Not only do patents make it possible to suppress the free exchange of information about the biological material, they also may cost patient lives because they slow time-sensitive research on life-threatening diseases.

Valerie Ng, past president of the Academy of Clinical Laboratory Physicians and Scientists, finds the exclusive licensing of gene patents antithetical to traditional medical research. "This is a break with the whole history of laboratory testing in which somebody develops a test and it's immediately available to the entire medical community," she says.[68]

Scientists and Doctors Against Life Patents

Scientists working on the same DNA as a patent holder of a disease gene will be delayed or will completely halt their own research. First, they may fear a lawsuit. A patent lawsuit costs a company an average of $1.5 million before awards are even adjudicated.[69] "For the highly innovative and usually underfunded companies that make up much of the biotech industry, the mere threat of patent litigation is enough to force them to shut down a production line or shutter the business itself," author Fred Warshofsky observed in his 1994 book, *The Patent Wars: The Battle to Own the World's Technology.*[70] Second, researchers may be forced to change their experiments significantly to comply with the patent-holding company's requirements and restrictions. Third, the royalties that the patent-holding company demands may make research prohibitively expensive.

In 1999, the biotech company Athena Diagnostics sent letters to laboratories informing them of Athena's newly awarded patent on an Alzheimer's disease genetic test. Athena demanded royalty payments that were twice the price charged by laboratories before the patent. "The cost put the test way beyond the researchers operating on government grants," *The Guardian* (London) reported.[71] As opposed to Athena Diagnostics, the government researchers were not using the test to make money. They were using the test to look for new mutations.

Even if the patentee owning a disease gene allows more than one company to study the gene, the cost can be exorbitant. Jonathan F. Tait, director of the Molecular Diagnosis Laboratory at the University of Washington, notes that "if a [company] offers nonexclusive licenses but it sets royalty terms unreasonably high, it can shut out other labs."[72]

The American College of Medical Genetics reacted to these patent enforcement techniques with a policy statement in

1999: "It is the ACMG's position that: 1) Genes and their mutations are naturally occurring substances that should not be patented. 2) Patents on genes with clinical implications must be very broadly licensed. 3) Licensing agreements should not limit access through excessive royalties and other unreasonable terms."[73]

Although not against all life patents, the American Medical Association states: "One of the goals of genetic research is to achieve better medical treatments and technologies. Granting patent protection should not hinder this goal."[74]

Public Money for Public Good

> Look at biotechnology. The basic discoveries that led to the field were based on decades of academic, publicly funded research. I believe that if these discoveries had been subject to proprietary control and restriction, we wouldn't have created the field of molecular biology.
> —Ronald R. Dederoff, director of
> the forest biotechnology group at
> North Carolina State University[75]

In 2002 alone, taxpayers gave over $23 billion to basic research in health and medicine.[76] This $23 billion includes only the funding for the National Institutes of Health. If one considers the budgets for other governmental entities such as the National Science Foundation, the Centers for Disease Control and Prevention, and the Department of Energy, this number is much higher.

And yet, with their life patents, the universities and companies that benefit from using this money stymie innovation in the ways described above and ultimately stand in the way of progress in medical science.

Meanwhile, the public expenditure is growing rapidly, already double in 2002 what it was just five years earlier. Overall, the 2002 budget for federal R&D was the largest dollar increase in history, up 13% from the year before.

"About 95% of the fundamental discoveries that point you in the right direction come out of basic science funded by government and not-for-profit sources," says Dr. C. Thomas Caskey, president of Merck's research institute.[77]

Public support comes in more ways than just money. Many biotech companies are led by scientists who got their training in publicly funded research. Universities that make millions of dollars on licensing their patents continue to enjoy non-profit status. Meanwhile, the government's genome project, and other projects like it, have freely and expediently shared their research results to stimulate technological advancement in the private sector.

In fact, the government sank $3 billion into the genome project precisely to stimulate and support the private sector. "An important feature of this [Human Genome] project is the federal government's long standing dedication to the transfer of technology to the private sector," the genome project's web page says. "By licensing technologies to private companies and awarding grants for innovative research, the project is catalyzing the multi-billion dollar U.S. biotechnology industry..."[78]

The web page does not mention the public's health. The closest it comes to mentioning anything resembling the public good is when it states that the project may foster "the development of new medical applications."[79]

Public support of the biotech and drug industries is not necessarily a bad thing. A healthy biotech industry is important for the U.S. economy, as is a healthy pharmaceutical industry. We want our industries to be strong and competitive. But the public deserves to have some control over the research it finances. After all, it's our money. That control should include demanding that upstream knowledge be shared openly. By mandating this, a real gold rush may happen in which preventions and cures are discovered.

A brief look at how the public has funded some of the discoveries presented in this chapter demonstrates the lack of bang we're getting for our buck.

In its analysis of tuberculosis, the Institute of Medicine agrees with the pharmaceutical companies' estimate that it would cost $350 million to develop and bring a new tuberculosis drug to market. That price is reflective of the total cost of R&D and includes the research that went into other drugs the company worked on that have failed and did not come to market. But the government already spends an enormous amount of money and resources researching tuberculosis. Because the expensive basic research has already been done, the Institute of Medicine estimates that the true cost of developing drugs against tuberculosis for private companies is quite low, "probably in the range of $15 to $30 million."[80]

Myriad's BRCA patents were built on years of work by the National Institutes of Health and scientists working in government-funded research throughout the world.

The discovery that CCR5 plays an important role in the AIDS virus was made by groups of government-funded scientists. Now one company reaps the benefits.

After years of public investment in these areas, why is the knowledge about pathogens and genes now kept hidden and restricted from other researchers?

The United States government, even while pursuing scientific discoveries within its own laboratories, has long held the policy of working with private industry to advance scientific knowledge. Academic institutions often sought both public and private money to fund their research. Each of the partners— industry, government, universities, institutions, and the individual scientists—together pursued nature's riddles. Ideally, the combined motives of commercial gain, scientific ambition, and public good can give scientific advancement a balance of power.

In 1980, Congress passed the Bayh-Dole Act that changed all that. The act enabled universities and other publicly funded research organizations to patent their discoveries and then license the patents to industry for royalties.[81] Two elements of the act revolutionized the effect of industry on nonprofit scientific research: One, universities and other non-profit organizations could take publicly funded research results and license them to a single company exclusively. Two, researchers in nonprofit environments could now personally profit from licensing the patents.

As a result, the majority of human DNA patents have been awarded to "non-profit" and often publicly supported universities. They in turn, license them exclusively to single companies. From these licensing contracts, universities and their researchers make millions.

In other words, the very institutions built with public money are joining the fight to lock up intellectual property. "Universities have established sometimes aggressive and usually expensive offices to protect intellectual property, including research tools," Harold Varmus, president of the Memorial Sloan-Kettering Cancer Center, told Congress. "Companies and universities have sometimes employed onerous licensing terms, even for academic investigators. Ideas and materials have been less openly exchanged in many well-documented situations."[82]

To the chagrin of many life scientists in academia, government, and industry itself, the balance has now tipped toward the pursuit of profit over all other gains. In the last fifteen years, the goals of biotechnology have changed because of university and governmental ties to private industry. Academics are no longer satisfied with having their name on journal articles declaring scientific breakthroughs. Only after biotech companies send their research results to newspapers to be declared "genetic discoveries" are the results offered to fellow scientists in order to be tested and confirmed. Sequana Therapeutics Inc. distributed a press release in 1997 of their "genetic breakthrough" on a new "asthma gene" without publishing the experiments in journals for other scientists to confirm. Sequana's press release contained little scientific data but mentioned that the company would receive a $2 million "milestone payment" from its corporate partner because of the announcement. When pressed, Sequana admitted they were not ready to produce an actual scientific report.[83]

For companies or universities that have life patents, drugs and cures aren't necessary for short term profits. In many cases, the patent itself is the product. If a company or university has patented a particular sequence of DNA, it can be in the business of merely selling or licensing that patent. In other words, your job is done once you have won a patent. Leave it to other people, who are paying you royalties, to figure out what the DNA actually does.

In 1993, U.S. companies earned more than $60 billion from patent royalties.[84] In *The Patent Wars*, Warshofsky describes the growing economic weight given to patents themselves, completely separate from an useful "invention" that they describe: "In fields such as electronics, communications, biotechnology, and still-developing technologies such as superconductivity, the wealth of the world is generated. Trillions of dollars, millions of jobs, and economic and geopolitical power all stem from ideas rather than raw materials or factories as they once did." Warshofsky estimates that in 1994 intellectual property made up over 50 percent of all American exports.

Patent litigation is another area where companies can make money from patents themselves without ever having to build the invention they describe. "In the decade from 1980 to 1990, patent litigation has mushroomed by 52 percent," Warshofsky writes. "In some fields like biotechnology, for example, legal briefs outweigh scientific papers by orders of magnitude, and lawyers are as eagerly sought as PhDs."

Patent infringement lawsuits clearly slow down the time it takes for important scientific breakthroughs to be made public. Patent lawsuits especially affect the research of smaller companies, where much of the real innovation happens. In Chapter four, we will examine more closely the effect that patent litigations have on the actual economies of biotechnology and pharmaceutical companies. Patent litigation taxes the public as well in terms of judges' and staff salaries, facilities maintenance, providing for juries, and other courtroom costs for cases that can continue for months. But most importantly, patent litigation slows down innovation that could be helping medical research.

While nearly all researchers, lawyers, and businessmen agree that intellectual property rights should be protected in some way in order to stimulate U.S. inventiveness, they by no means agree that the patent system actually does this. Even some biotech companies realize the mess created by our current patent system. "There should be no patenting of gene sequences, period. They were invented by nature," Barbara Caulfield, a lawyer for the biotechnology company Affymetrix Corp., told the Federal Trade Commission. "This is a position Affymetrix feels strongly about."[85]

Using the System to Fight the System

The U.S. Patent Office doesn't recognize the discoveries of scientists like Mary-Claire King or those that found the CCR5/AIDS link. Nor will it protect families like the Greenbergs from exploitation for economic gain. Given this context, some have taken to extraordinary means to preserve the integrity of research on genes.

As in the case of the families of children with Canavan disease, support groups for specific diseases have witnessed first hand how patents slow down research on diseases that affect them directly. In 1994, the parents of Elizabeth and Ian Terry discovered that their children suffered from a rare genetic disease called *pseudoxanthoma elasticum* or PXE. Symptoms of PXE include blindness and deteriorating blood vessels in the stomach and heart. The symptoms would not appear until early adulthood, however, and Ian and Elizabeth were still only five and seven respectively.[86] The parents held out some hope that a disparate group of individual researchers that had suddenly become interested in their children's condition might find a cure in time.

"We quickly realized the research community was not set up to work together," Sharon Terry told *The American Lawyer*. "We said, 'we're not giving our kids' blood.'"

Instead, the Terrys contacted other families with the condition and developed a blood and tissue bank. With the help of lawyer friends, they founded the PXE International Inc. and have begun filing for their own patents that would protect the DNA of PXE families. When it comes time for PXE International to license their patents out for research, Sharon Terry is clear about their motives: "We're not as hard-nosed about profits. We're more interested in the search for treatments and patient support and research."[87]

Support groups for autism and diabetes have followed PXE International and are starting to pool their biological resources as well.

Life patents so angered a British poet and waitress named Donna MacLean, that she sent the U.K. patent office a letter asking that she patent herself. "There's a kind of unpleasant, grasping, greedy atmosphere at the moment around the mapping of the human genome," MacLean said. "I wanted to see if a human being could protect their own genes in law."

"It has taken 30 years of hard labor for me to discover and invent myself," MacLean wrote in her patent application, "and now I wish to protect my invention from unauthorized exploitation, genetic or otherwise."

MacLean's rather tongue-in-cheek request for a patent may actually be granted. Her application has been given a number, GB0000180.0, and is being considered. *The Guardian* reported that "Brian Caswell, assistant director of marketing at the UK patent office, would not rule out the possibility that a cunningly-worded patent application for a human being might be acceptable."[88]

While groups like PXE International and people like MacLean find ways to work within the patent system to protect their genetic heritage, this is an impossibility for farmers, indigenous people and other populations around the globe. In the next chapter, we will see how life patents are endangering the world's food, enabling companies and universities to steal cultural artifacts, and allowing the theft of genes from entire populations.

CHAPTER TWO

Raping the Land, Reaping the People

Patents and Biocolonialism

> Put baldly, patents are killing people. But that's not all. Intellectual property protection has become a tool to make permanent the growing inequality of the global economy: the rich get richer and the poor get poorer. Drugs are only the most blatant example of how, through TRIPs, the developed countries have stacked the odds in their favor. They have set the ground rules for the knowledge economy so they can extract a constant flow of income from less developed countries.
>
> —Madeleine Bunting, columnist, *The Guardian* (UK)[1]

On December 12, 1990, the United States Department of Agriculture joined up with the agrochemical corporation W.R. Grace to apply for a European patent on a fascinating extract that they claimed to have invented. The extract was found not only to be a natural fungicide on plants, but also appeared to have medicinal value for humans as well. The patent was awarded in 1994 and, over the next decade, more than 90 additional patents on the extract were awarded.

The extract appeared to be not only a brilliant scientific "invention," it also promised a number of successful products. A pesticide created without synthetic chemicals and factories would please the environmental movement. The homeopathic market in vogue in Europe and the U.S. would be attracted to the extract because it was a "natural" medicine and did not need to be altered in any way from its natural form. The monopoly on the extract, assured by the patent system, promised to be a financial mother lode for W.R. Grace.

The problem with this "invention" is that millions of people are aware of the extract and have been using it for at least two thousand years. The extract, taken from a tree found in India called neem, has been used throughout Indian history in many ways, including—surprise!—as a natural pesticide and a medicine, as well as for veterinary care and in toiletries and cosmetics. Neem is mentioned in 2000-year-old Indian literature and venerated in the country's art, religion, and culture. Scientifically, it has been analyzed by Indian researchers and commercial interests for decades.[2]

With a patent on neem, W.R. Grace would be allowed to develop and sell products from a biological component that has been freely shared for millennia. In theory, if the Indian government ever agreed to enforce U.S. style patents that cover biological material, W.R. Grace could file patent infringement suits on all Indians who sell neem commercially as well as those who study it in scientific and medical experiments.

As is often the case with life patents, the Indian public was unaware that someone was claiming ownership of neem until after the patent was awarded. Vandana Shiva, an Indian physicist and director of the Research Foundation for Science, Technology and Natural Resource Policy, happened to read about the patent in a journal. She publicized the patent, organized protestors, and filed a patent challenge in 1995. In May of 2000, after a five-year campaign involving other non-profits and farmers' rights groups, Shiva and her team succeeded in repealing the patent.[3]

"TRIPs [Trade Related International Property Rights Agreement] and U.S.-style patent laws annihilate the rights of Third World communities by not having any system of recognition and protection of indigenous knowledge," Shiva writes.

"Biopiracy is intellectual and cultural rape."

Nearly every indigenous group throughout the world has, or will soon have, a Western company or government trying to mine its genetic heritage through patents on human genes, plants and seeds, and cultural knowledge. Mexican beans, South Asian basmati rice, and African cattle all have been subject to intellectual property claims. As well, human genes have been "mined" in the hope that pharmaceuticals can be developed from them. Genes have been prospected from the inhabitants of Tristan da Cunha (a South Atlantic island), the Pima Indians of Arizona, Chinese villages, the Hagahai people of Papua New Guinea, and the entire population of Iceland.

Why indigenous cultures? The theory behind mining a certain indigenous people's genes is that the population is more genetically similar or homogenous than people living in the general population. For example, the inhabitants of Tristan da Cunha are all descendents of a few sailors that settled or were shipwrecked there in the early 1800s. The 300 people that now live on the island are all products of intermarriage between those early settlers. Some geneticists believe that with such an isolated community, correlations can be drawn between the characteristics of their genes (genotype) and their physical characteristics and conditions (phenotype). In the case of Tristan da Cunha, a third of the population suffers from asthma. By analyzing the genotypes of the population of Tristan da Cunha, scientists hope to discover the genetic causes of asthma. The idea of a truly genetically homogenous culture of human beings—even as isolated as the Tristan da Cunha people—is currently being debated within the scientific community. Nevertheless, many corporations are betting their stocks on the idea.

Indigenous cultures have also served as an historical source for foodstuffs and medicinal plants. There are over 20,000 species of medicinal plants in use today. Knowledge of foods and these medicinal plants has been passed down for generations in indigenous cultures, often because of their tight family structures and their relative isolation. Through life patents, corporations can now claim exclusive ownership over the knowledge—and may turn around and charge the very people who developed the food and medicine for its use.

In many cases, it is not simply a plant or a drop of blood that is being taken and its biological components claimed as "invented," it is also an important symbol of a culture's history and heritage. Foodstuffs, medicinal plants, and an individual's blood may be considered sacred and central to a culture's religious sensibilities.

"Some indigenous people say the patenting of this plant is the equivalent of somebody in their group patenting the Christian cross," said David Rothschild of the Coalition for Amazonian Peoples and their Environment. Rothschild was referring to the patent awarded to a United States researcher in 1986 on an Amazonian plant called ayahuasca. For the researcher, the ayahuasca contained interesting medicinal elements. For tribes in the Amazon, the plant held spiritual significance. "It's also offensive to them that someone in the U.S. is claiming the intellectual property of the knowledge of this plant, which they see as being theirs."[4]

Certain foodstuffs are not just staples in a people's diet, they can also be essential elements in a people's cosmology. In response to over 600 patents that have been granted on rice, including patents on rice genes, plants, and breeding methods, a coalition of people's groups and nongovernmental organizations across Asia released this statement: "Rice means life to us in Asia. It is the cornerstone of our food systems, our languages, our cultures and our livelihoods for thousands of years... IPRs [intellectual property rights] on rice give companies immoral and unethical monopoly control and force farmers to pay for the use of genetic resources and knowledge which originated from them..."[5]

Through what Shiva calls "biopiracy" and "biocolonialism," U.S. patent laws are fast becoming the standard around which international property laws are created.

Ironically, the first person to use the word "patent" in the American context was Christopher Columbus. Columbus used "patent" to describe the ownership—and the rights that came with that ownership—that he claimed on the lands he discovered.[6] This patenting of the New World meant that he claimed the land, the people, and all the resources for a far away Western European country to exploit. The Europeans were able to sustain these exploitive patents over indigenous lands and peoples simply because they had the military strength to enforce them. Their "goodwill" excuse for doing so was the promotion of Christianity, though this was simply a cloak for power and greed.

Like the old kings and queens of Europe, U.S. companies and multinational corporations use their economic strength to push for international protection of patent rights. Their "goodwill" excuse is the promotion of science and medicine. But their motives are power and greed and the consequence is exploitation.

Companies are actively patenting human biological material as well as animals and plants. But the most aggressive and the most frightening movement is the rush to patent the seeds and foodstuffs of the world. Patenting plants and seeds not only restricts research, it creates monopolies and monocultures that threaten the world's food sources.

"Pass the Corn, It's Mine." Ownership of Food

> The things that give us a safe and healthy food supply are slowly eroding. It's a slow death.
> —Dr. Samuel H. Smith, former President
> of Washington State University[7]

Diamond v. Chakrabarty, the 1980 Supreme Court decision that opened the flood gates on life patents, established that genetically altered microorganisms could be patented. Since then, as we will see, the flood has increased and the Patent Office now allows genetically altered plants and mammals to be patented. In Chapter Five we will look more closely at patents on genetically altered plants and animals. But, as in Chapter One, the patents in this chapter are patents on plants and food-stuffs *as they are found in nature*. The Patent Office has allowed this for the last decade and in December 2001, the Supreme Court upheld the practice of granting patents on seeds and plants whose genetic make-up is indistinguishable from their natural biological state.[8] Put simply, the Court allowed the companies to continue to rip-off nature. Since 1980, at least 1,800 patents on plants, plant parts, and seeds have been granted by the Patent Office.[9]

In 1994, two researchers at the University of Colorado received a patent for a high-yield cereal that was naturally high in protein. With no genetic alteration or hybridization, the food-stuff could tolerate high altitudes, dry climates, and poor soil. The Colorado team promised that they would soon seek commercial production of the healthy grain. With the patent, the researchers would have the right to prevent anyone else from making, using or selling the cereal without permission or royalties.

The cereal "invented" by the Colorado researchers had been called *quinoa* for centuries by farmers in Bolivia and Ecuador. The researchers admitted that they had "just picked it up" on a trip to South America. *Quinoa* is an important element of the diet of indigenous people throughout the Andes, as well as an important export for Bolivia. Consumption of the Bolivian *quinoa* in the United States has grown to $1 billion a year.[10]

If commercial production began in the United States as the Colorado researchers proposed, it would dramatically cut into South American exports of the cereal. The patent could keep Bolivia from selling the *quinoa* internationally and even to its own people if it was enforced. Agricultural agencies again organized and prepared for a costly court battle. They promised to include an analysis of the patent by scientists that would prove that the cereal was an exact copy of the South American product.

The two researchers reportedly wanted to save the embarrassment of an international trial and dropped the patent in 1998.

"This is such a relief. *Quinoa* is the meat of the Andes," said Jaime Bravo, a Bolivian representative who fought the patent. "It was almost stolen from us."[11]

"We won on *quinoa*," Alejandro Argumedo, coordinator of the Indigenous Peoples' Biodiversity Network said. "But there are still more than 120 proprietary claims on indigenous crops and plants," he said. "It amounts to a massive abuse of intellectual property laws and a wholesale piracy of the knowledge of indigenous people."[12]

The neo-liberal ideal in economics, reflected in the World Trade Organization and in international agreements, is the hope that the world market will become completely open. The idea of open, free trade means that all countries will have equal opportunity to produce products and export them, free of tariffs, special taxes, or other import/export obstacles. Consumers throughout the world would then be given a chance to choose equally among competitive products depending on quality and the "real" price.

But when organizations and companies in the U.S. steal another country's product, claim that they "invented" it, and then shut down the other country's production by way of international property right protection, the much heralded open competition ceases to exist.

Nutritionless Food and the Potatoe Famine: The Cost of Monocultures and Monopolies

Twenty years ago, there were 7,000 sources for seeds throughout the world. Companies, universities, farmers, and agricultural cooperatives developed, produced, and sold seeds. Now, ten seed companies own a third of the world's commercial market and they are quickly moving to control it all.[13] These broad monopolies have been largely achieved by using the U.S. patent system as a tool to gain control of whole species of plants and seeds. Much of the production and selling of seeds worldwide is now in the hands of the five largest companies: Pharmacia, Syngenta, DuPont, Dow Chemical, and Aventis.

The patent monopoly on seeds and foodstuffs affects developing and developed countries alike. Life patents not only allow control of the products produced, i.e. the world's food, they also restrict research on seeds and foodstuffs. A 2001 Department of Agriculture analysis reported that private sector research and development on plant breeding had increased significantly due to changes in science and the patent protection for plants. In the meantime, however, "public sector agriculture in general, and public plant breeding in particular, is in trouble in both industrialized and developing nations."[14] Another report found that 45% of plant researchers in United States universities have reported that companies have interfered with their research because of property rights.[15]

"Society benefits when there is public access to scientific knowledge that, when developed by the private sector, is subject to intellectual property rights," the Department of Agriculture report stated.[16] The report emphasized the need to save public research because it fostered "greater sharing of information and more work on traits on plant varieties (such as environmental suitability and nutritional characteristics) that may be under-researched by private breeding programs."

As opposed to research in the private sector, public research takes the time to study a food's nutritional value and analyzes whether the plants can survive certain environments. These "clear public good components," the report says, are markedly missing from private sector research. The reason why nutritional value and environmental suitability is not studied by the private sector is made clear in the report's summary: "[Public sector research conducts] long-term research, which private

firms may avoid in their desire to earn profits in the near term."
By allowing life patents to be used to restrict research on the
world's foodstuffs, we are creating a future where our food will
be less nutritional than it is marketable. As well, our foodstuffs
will also be less able to survive in changing environmental conditions.

In addition, the report directly contradicts industry's claim
that life patents stimulate scientific research: "[Public sector
research furthers] scientific knowledge, which may be a 'public
good' or benefit to society as a whole, but may not be a major
research goal of private firms if it is not financially profitable."[17]

The monopolies of seed companies are strengthened by
other movements to protect industries and take away farmers'
rights by using patent protection. In 1994, Congress passed a bill
that made it illegal for U.S. farmers to sell or save seeds that were
protected by patents.[18] After harvesting a crop, farmers could not
save patented seeds for the next year or sell or trade seeds to their
neighbors. The law not only successfully snuffed out a tradition
honored for centuries as part of farming, it might also be considered an invasion of a farmer's property and privacy.

It is as if you were told, every time you went to the store
to buy food or a stereo or a CD, the company that held patents
on those products could control what you did with them in your
own home. After you paid good money for the products, you
were instructed that you would be sued if too many people
shared the food, if you turned and sold the stereo at a garage
sale, or if too many people listened to the CD. Even after you
paid for the products, you do not legally own them. They are
owned forever by a company. One contract between a seed
company and a farmers' group even stipulated that the company could send observers on the farmers' property to watch what
was done with the seeds.[19]

Plants and seeds are different from food or CDs, however,
in that plants and seeds are growing, multiplying, organic things
and prone to unpredictable behavior. The Monsanto

Corporation is currently suing a Canadian farmer whose farm, the company discovered, was producing corn that came from the company's patented seeds. The farmer, Percy Schmeiser, insists that the seeds blew onto his land and he had no idea that they were "Monsanto's seeds." Monsanto is suing Schmeiser for $170,000.

Angela Rickman, campaign co-ordinator with the Sierra Club of Canada, explained the importance of the Schmeiser case. " It is very important for small farmers, not just in Canada but around the world, who are really concerned with the ability of multinationals to patent what was previously considered to be the genetic common. The whole world will be watching the outcome."[20]

The case is expected to be heard by the Canadian Supreme Court in late 2003.

Both domestically and internationally, agrochemical companies are using the patent system to create monopolies that are not only unjust to individual farmers and cultures; they are also a risk to the world's food source. If only a few companies control the seeds that are used to grow our foodstuffs, there is great danger of monoculture—the mass production of genetically uniform crops. In their book *Genetically Engineered Food: Changing the Nature of Nature*, Martin Teitel and Kimberly Wilson write:

> By modifying plants under carefully controlled laboratory conditions and then setting up a strict regime of chemical-based cultivation in the field, companies can ensure the genetic uniformity of purebred, high-yield varieties. The plants that result from this process are highly invariable, not only in their appearance and yield, but also in their genes. If the genes are virtually the same, the diversity that we need to maintain ecological and planetary health is diminished… Rather, what makes good agricultural and ecological sense is to plant as many varieties as we can to maximize biodiversity and minimize monoculture.[21]

Teitel and Wilson point to the Irish potato famine of the 19th century as an example of what happens when a community becomes dependent on a single crop variety.

Biocolonialism is sometimes regarded as a North-South tension where U.S. universities and companies nearly always come out the bad guys. When one considers that 95% of the world's species of plants and animals are in the Southern Hemisphere, and yet only a very small minority of life patents have been claimed by companies or countries located below the equator, serious questions of ownership arise. How is it that U.S. property rights are being claimed on material that isn't even found in our own backyards?

But the North-South dichotomy is perhaps too simplistic. Rather, the controversies surrounding life patents that cover indigenous plants and foodstuffs is one where the wealthy and powerful are pitted against groups that have historically been marginalized or their voices ignored, wherever the country.

Here in the United States, private interests use research as an excuse to monopolize indigenous foodstuffs. The University of Minnesota has mapped the genome for wild rice because, researchers there say, it is "important as a foundation for genetic and crop improvement studies."[22]

The Minnesota Chippewa Tribe, which has harvested wild rice for centuries, view the university's research as a profit-motivated attempt to monopolize a foodstuff that is a cultural cornerstone of their people.

Minnesota Chippewa Tribe President Norman Deschampe told his tribe, "The genetic variants of wild rice found naturally occurring on the waters in the territories ceded by the Minnesota Chippewa Tribe to the State of Minnesota are a unique treasure that has been carefully protected by the people of our tribe for centuries."

"While the future uses of such scientific data are at present unknown, it is relatively assured as to who will most likely reap the benefits of this knowledge," Native American activist

Winona LaDuke observed in regard to the University of Minnesota's research. "The $21 million wild rice business is largely dominated by just a few paddy rice firms. Their interest in genetic work on wild rice stems largely from their own economic interests, not environmental, humanitarian, or tribal interests."[23]

LaDuke's suspicion concerning the motives of the University of Minnesota's researchers is given fuel by the fact that two of the researchers came from two of the five big seed companies, DuPont and Monsanto. Already, the company Norcal Wild Rice has successfully patented a domesticated wild rice.

But the Native Americans' fear goes beyond the idea that a company will patent a foodstuff and therefore attempt to control all of its commercial use. The real fear is that the rice will be genetically modified and natural wild rice will become extinct.

This is what has happened with corn in Chiapas, Mexico. In the spring of 2002, it was discovered that the indigenous corn varieties of the region were contaminated by genetically engineered corn. The dangers of genetically engineered seeds and foodstuffs, as we will see, are still being debated scientifically, but the fact is that a centuries-old foodstuff has disappeared forever because of financially-motivated tinkering with nature.

The corn of Chiapas and the wild rice of Minnesota are not merely foodstuffs for a specific group of people. Corn and wild rice are not only spiritually and economically important to certain marginalized tribes. They are a natural resource and heritage for all of us.

So why don't indigenous people or developing countries simply start to patent their seeds, foodstuffs, medicinal herbs, and even their people's own genes? Why not protect and even make money from their genetic heritage in the same way U.S. companies do?

Clearly, these groups are highly outgunned by their corporate and state-funded counterparts in wealthy countries. Indigenous groups don't have nearly enough financial, technological, or human resources. Developing countries are under increasing pressure both domestically and internationally to allow Western corporate expansion—and with them U.S. patent policies—into their countries. They do not have the legal power or money to sustain long patent infringement cases that are endemic to the intellectual property rights game. Research institutions in poorer countries do not have the government subsidies or the immense amount of taxpayer's money that support U.S., European, and Australian universities and corporations. These are all inequalities that have emerged within the more general context of globalization and free trade.

But there is also a philosophical difference that has emerged between the wealthy multi-national corporations and indigenous groups concerning biological resources, seeds that have freely reproduced for centuries, natural medicines that have been passed down through generations, and even the molecules found in human bodies. Many critics in indigenous cultures decry life patents because they believe nature, and knowledge about nature, should be owned and shared by everyone. Biological material is a common heritage, they say, a common responsibility that belongs to all human beings. While one may be allowed to buy and sell the plants and seeds that are produced on one's land worked with one's own hands, one should not be able to restrict others from doing the same on their land. For many critics, when a Western company says that it has "invented" and therefore owns a medicinal plant or a type of corn, it robs nature of its dignity. It also robs all human beings of their common property.

Harvesting Humans : Genetic Databases

At least the modern Icelanders' Viking ancestors

made no pretense that their raids and piratical activities
were in the public interest.

—R.C. Lewontin[24]

On December 17, 1998 the Icelandic Parliament passed a
law that would allow a private company access to all its citizens'
personal medical records and genetic data. The company,
deCode Genetics, set up with U.S. money, had million dollar
deals already in place with pharmaceutical and insurance companies.

The reason for the development of the Iceland Health
Database was explicitly given by the Iceland Parliament: the
country hoped to diversify its economic base by becoming
involved in the biotechnology industry. Iceland's economy currently relies heavily on the fishing industry that provides 70%
of its export earnings, yet only employs 12% of Iceland's
280,000 people. Despite its reliance on the fishing industry,
Iceland has a strong economy, with only 2.7% unemployment
and an extensive welfare system.

By matching the health records with genetic characteristics of such a large and theoretically homogenous population,
deCode hopes to discover patterns of health that match genetic variations.[25] To date, deCode has applied for patents on 350
molecular components taken from Icelanders that it has
claimed to tie to 40 common diseases.[26]

Human genetic databases have been developed before, but
the Iceland database represents the largest ever attempted.
Health records can be easily collected and standardized in
Iceland because of its centralized national health care system.
Records from as far back as 1950 will be collected for the database. As well, blood samples will be taken on each citizen's visit
to their health care provider and entered into the database to be
tested for their genetic make-up.

All Icelandic citizens are automatically included in the
database. A citizen may opt to withdraw themselves from the

study but must fill out a complicated form in order to do so. All children under the age of eighteen at the time the database becomes functional are automatically included, unless their parents remove them by way of the opt-out form. Wards of the state, including children, disabled, and other individuals, and the records of deceased Icelanders will be automatically entered into the database.

Currently, the database is embroiled in lawsuits and fierce public debates, both scientific and ethical, and the whole project has been stalled. Part of the controversy lies in the fact that citizens are automatically entered into the database without consent forms. People only fill out forms if they do not wish to participate. Further, citizens are not allowed to withdraw from the database at all after a certain point in its development. These two elements of the database have drawn criticism from a large number of international and domestic professional organizations and human rights advocates. Automatic participation and not allowing individuals the right to withdraw from the database bring into question whether "informed consent" is properly being given to the citizens of Iceland. In essence, the critics say, the Iceland database is a giant medical experiment, one of the largest ever proposed and the right to refuse to participate in a medical experiment is a basic human right.

"It has been heavily criticized that there is no provision in the law for individuals to withdraw their data from the database," Dr. Tomas Soega of the National University Hospital in Reykjavik and Dr. Bogi Andersen of the University of California write. "This is a blatant violation of a basic human right as clearly stated in item 9 of the Nuremberg Code... In summary, the database law is based on a new ethical paradigm for research, specifically adapted for commercial purposes, but with poor demonstration of scientific benefit. According to this ideology, traditional ethics instruments such as the Helsinki declaration and recommendations of the American Society for Human Genetics do not apply to genetics research in

Iceland."[27]

Even if there is no corporal harm to participants in medical experiments, the philosophy behind allowing individuals the choice of participating in studies or not is that it is a basic human right to participate in what one chooses, with the private or public institutions one chooses. Reasons for choosing not to participate include discrepancies in belief or philosophy of the institution running an experiment. An obvious example would be an experiment run by a government, a religiously-based organization with motives or philosophies that don't agree with yours, or by a company with profit motives.

"These ideas show total disregard for individual autonomy," Soega and Andersen write. "It should be left up to each individual, not the government, to determine whether he/she wants to restrict his/her medical records for research and/or commercial purposes."

"The main issue is whether people [who donate samples to genetic databases] know what they're getting into," says Boston University law professor George J. Annas.[28]

Although the majority of Icelanders will have at least one chance to "opt out" of being a part of the database, some Icelanders will not even be given this minimal amount of "consent." Children's voices have been completely silenced in consideration of the database, since children must rely on adults to fill out the complicated "opt-out" form. Otherwise, they are automatically admitted into the database and cannot withdraw even when they become adults. The physically and mentally disabled are also given no chance of consent or withdrawal, as their DNA is controlled by state- or family-appointed guardians. Information from deceased Icelanders is entered automatically despite any contrary wishes by the relatives or kin of the deceased.

The Iceland Health Database is unique because of its size and the cooperation of the hosting government—i.e., its "legality." But the idea of "mining" a population for its genes in the hopes of discovering a pattern that matches health to genetic make-up is not new. Nor is the idea that the genetic make-up of a population can be turned into intellectual property to be bought and sold like raw resources.

In the past ten years, many companies and governments have been accused of human rights violations, mostly in terms of consent, when they have conducted smaller, less publicized medical trials on populations with the intention of obtaining property rights on molecular material. In many cases, the genetic information taken from these populations is sold for millions of dollars to corporations without the permission or even knowledge of the people it was taken from.

In nearly every case, the medical trials on a populations' DNA were conducted by Western corporations or governments on poorer, less educated populations. As John Pomfret and Deborah Nelson reported in *The Washington Post*, poverty-stricken individuals in dire need of medical attention are the victims of numerous injustices caused by Western pharmaceutical and biotech companies. For example, researchers looking to establish a genetic database like that of Iceland exploited Chinese villagers. The reporters found that the individual villagers used for the research were often pressured by the Chinese government to cooperate with the Western researchers, thus rendering the idea of consent ridiculous:

> "If they don't want to participate," said one doctor, "officials go down to the villages and do thought work and move them to participate."
>
> 'Thought work' involves meetings with local government and party officials and can involve both subtle and blatant forms of pressure. If officials are having trouble rounding up test subjects, residents said, thought work can become heavy-handed, even coercive. Residents rely on the Communist Party and local government for many favors involving taxes and the division of land. Families who are not cooperative could suffer, residents said.[29]

The medical researchers were funded by Harvard University and its sponsor Millennium Pharmaceuticals, Inc.

People with Bad Genes Need Not Apply: Genetic Discrimination

A good reason *not* to participate in Iceland's database and other genetic databases is the threat of genetic discrimination. In the Iceland debate, "women raised again and again their concerns for the psychological as well as the physical well-being of their family members."[30] Among other things, the Iceland women feared genetic discrimination that might result from the project's study of breast cancer, one of deCode's proposed areas of analysis. This worry was compounded greatly by the fact that deCode hoped to sell the database's information to insurance companies. The fear of genetic profiling is founded in reality, as we will see in the next chapter, and Iceland currently has no laws against genetic discrimination.

The fear is heightened by the fact that the guarantee of confidentiality that organizers of the Iceland database have promised has come under considerable fire from electronic experts and citizens alike. A British computer safety expert hired by the Icelandic Medical Association concluded that the database's "privacy protection… falls well short of the minimum standards demanded elsewhere in the developed world."[31]

Another ironic "technical" problem with the confidentiality of the database derives from the fact that the DNA is being collected from real humans with complex relationships beyond their genetic codes. Iceland is a small, close-knit country and anyone hired to enter health records and genetic data into the system may know the people or families involved.

Kari Stefansson, the founder of the database, promises that it will usher in the "new genetics" wherein preventive medicine is "practiced through patient education and screening tests."[32] He adds that the database will go "hand in hand with healthcare delivery, which aims to increase access to excellent care at reasonable costs that society can afford." These words—screening tests, preventive medicine, and reasonable costs—translate to a program of eugenics for those who know that their physical and mental conditions, or the conditions of their children or their ancestors, are often considered unhealthy and expensive by society, governments, and insurance companies.

The New Wealth of Nations: DNA as Natural Resource

Molecular biology and one's genetic heritage is difficult to understand in terms of material property or a society's natural resource. Aside from a blood sample, nothing is physically taken from an individual by having their genetic structures tested and analyzed. As a material resource, the Icelanders' and the Chinese villagers' molecular make-up is not being depleted in the same sense that natural resources such as oil, lumber, and water are being depleted in other parts of the world.

However, DNA can be considered a material resource in the sense that it is bought and sold in the same way as those depletable natural resources. *The Washington Post* report quoted the lead researcher in the Chinese experiments as saying that the villager's DNA "was more valuable than gold."[33] Like gold, genetic information can be sold for money. Like gold, it's important to define who holds the claim or stake on the resources. Most would agree that unless rights to the resources are expressly sold off, the gold belongs to the land-holder. In the same way, the DNA belongs to the individual or the tribe or the group. In Iceland, parallels have been drawn between the country's genetic resources and its fishing and oil resources. Proponents of Iceland's database describe the genetic resources of Iceland as something that needs to be monetized for the good of the country: "What [deCode] wants to do is to 'make value' of these untapped resources, in consequence tapping such national information resources becomes a moral and national duty," Hilary Rose wrote in a report on the database for the Wellcome Trust.[34]

When molecular biology is considered a natural resource, then countries or individuals should be paid for the use of that resource. There are many "piracy" cases in the context of developing countries where payment or in-kind medical assistance has not been provided. Even in the Iceland example, the people and the government of a wealthy and educated country do not seem to be getting their money's worth.

"To us, the financial aspects of the arrangements surrounding this proposal appear to be strongly weighted against the people of Iceland," Stanford law professor Henry T. Greely and geneticist Mary-Claire King wrote to the government of Iceland. In essence, Greely and King said, Icelanders would only profit from the database in two rather dubious ways:

- They would benefit from any new drugs that were developed from the database. Given the current state of biotechnology and drug research, it is doubtful that new drugs will be forthcoming, at least as a direct result of the database.
- New jobs would open up in Iceland to support the database. Unfortunately, as the database will ultimately be in the form of electronically stored information, there is little reason for the database, and any people that it employs, to be located in any specific geographic location. Given Iceland's high cost of living, it is more likely that any industry developed around the database will be moved to a location where labor is cheaper.[35]

Sveinn Gudmundsson, the manager of the blood bank in Reykjavik, sees this as a real threat: "What haunts me about all this is that we have a huge pharmaceutical company involved here that has no real ties to Iceland and could someday just move on to some other small country."[36]

In addition to the lack of monetary payment or medical assistance in return for their "natural resource," Icelanders will lose all control of how this material resource will ultimately be used, just like the families of the children with Canavan disease where patent holders cut off rather than promoted promising research into possible cures. Although the database is now under the ideological pretense of acting as a vehicle to discover genetic cures for diseases, there are no laws which keep the database from being sold to insurance companies, HMOs, law enforcement databases, or used to create genetic screen tests.

As commodities, no one can say how the Icelandic or any human databases ultimately will be used. As private property, protected by patents, they can be sold to the highest bidder and the highest bidder can do with it what they please. This is exactly what happened to a human cell collection in Japan. The collection was gathered by a scientific organization that had subsequently used it as a collateral on a loan. In 2002, a court auctioned the cell collection off.[37]

The individual Icelander as well as Icelanders as a whole will not be asked if they agree morally with how their genes are being used. In fact, according to the founder of the database, Kari Stefansson, it is actually better if Icelanders knew less about what will happen to their genes: "It is enough that they understand their own desire to contribute to the advancement of science."[38]

Fools Gold in the Information Age

In the Iceland case, human DNA will be processed and codified into numbers and letters of statistical analysis. It will become analyzed and developed into a set of experimental "truths." In a word, they will become synthesized as knowledge or information.

But after all the investment of money and resources for such databases—and after the ethically questionable gathering of information—the actual scientific usefulness of the Icelandic or any genetic database is questionable. It may be fool's gold.

Scientists point out a number of problems with the database, and all such proposed genetic databases, that make their scientific relevancy suspect. In the first place, it is questionable whether Icelanders—or any group of people—are truly genetically homogenous; i.e. whether their genetic make-up is similar enough to draw scientific conclusions from. According to Einar Arnason, an Icelandic geneticist, Iceland "is not genetically pure, but rather one of the most genetically heterogeneous nations in Europe."[39]

In fact, there may be no such thing as genetic homogeneity within ethnicities or indigenous groups. Many scientists believe that there are just as many genetic differences between individuals as there are between races. Stephen O'Brien, chief of the Laboratory of Genomic Diversity at the National Cancer Institute puts it this way: "There's 10 times more difference between a white person and his Caucasian wife than between a white population and an African population."[40]

Thirdly, studies within one population or ethnicity have been shown to produce results that cannot be reproduced in other populations. "Susceptibility loci for complex diseases identified in one study population often cannot be replicated in other populations," Paula Kiberstis and Leslie Roberts wrote in an editorial in *Science*.[41]

The problem with genetic databases may be that the researchers studying them are more concerned with finding genetic cause for diseases, as opposed to looking for how the environment or lifestyles affect the genetic make-up and ultimately the health of a person. This may be why certain results from one population are not reproducible in other populations. It's not that their genes are different. But the mutation in a gene that may cause a health condition in one population may not cause the same health condition in another population because the lifestyles and environments are so different.

If this is so, then genetic databases will indeed be fool's gold. The answer to our health problems does not lie solely in our genes. In order to get a true understanding of disease, an individual's lifestyle and environment must be studied at the same time as the genes. Although part of the Icelandic database will be linked to medical records of individuals, the environmental and lifestyle factors will receive only a cursory investigation. Any detailed look into an Icelander's lifestyle and environment—including diet, exercise, sleeping habits, etc.— would, *de facto*, require that individuals be interviewed and studied much more than is possible in the context of the databases' promised secrecy and confidentiality. It is questionable whether in-depth "scientifically useful" queries can be asked of any database that must keep a certain level of confidentiality.

For many companies that are basing their futures on databases, like deCode, the hope lies not so much in producing cures or therapies, but in developing genetic tests from the databases. Genetic tests themselves appear to cause more harm than good, as we will see in Chapter five. But genetic tests that are developed from genetic databases are especially frightening because data from unchecked, scientifically-suspect research will produce "false positives," i.e. bungled test results.

In regard to the promises of genetic databases in general, Stanford Law School ethicist Henry Greely summed it up rather succinctly: "It's still mostly hype."[42]

Is there any scientific usefulness to genetic databases? Getting to this answer is again hindered by patents in the same way other research was stymied in Chapter one. The databases are bought and sold as commodities and, in many cases, only one company at a time will be allowed access to the information and only one company will be allowed to derive conclusions. In essence, the scientific method—testing a hypothesis—is lost when only one group of scientists is given access.

"The legislation appears to put data access under the power of a three person commission," Greely and King wrote in their letter to the government of Iceland. "By making an arrangement with a pharmaceutical company for the study of particular diseases, as it has done with Roche, DeCode could effectively block the commission from letting anyone else study the disease using the Icelandic database."[43]

"The conversion of this public resource [the database] into an exclusive commodity for a single company provides a terrible precedent for the rest of the world," Soega and Andersen say. "Ultimately, state-sponsored monopoly on access to research subjects will stand in the way of scientific progress."[44]

A good test for all genetic database research carried out overseas is the question of whether we would allow such research in the United States. If a private company came to Orange County and wanted to set up a database like Iceland's, would the American public stand for it? The answer is probably no. Yet, as in cases such as the families affected by Canavan disease, small scale versions of these exploitive experiments are already taking place here in the U.S.

An Apartheid of Patents

Developing countries lose out on both sides of patent law. While isolated populations are prospected for human genes and plant life, they rarely benefit from the technologies developed from them. In many instances, international patent law, enforced through such treaties as the World Trade Organization's (WTO) Agreement on Trade-Related Aspects of Intellectual Property Rights (TRIPs), creates an impossible trap for developing countries. Not only are developing countries and indigenous peoples "mined" for their genes and medicinal knowledge, they will also ultimately have little access to the technologies or drugs developed from their genetic heritage.

As mentioned earlier, the California company Sequana (now Axys Pharmaceuticals) owns the genetic make-up of the entire human population of Tristan da Cunha. The company has made a $70 million deal with the pharmaceutical company Boehringer Ingelheim to research the population's blood in hopes of finding therapies for asthma. When researchers visited the island in 1993, the residents of Tristan da Cunha had no idea that their blood would be turned into a commercial commodity. In a move reminiscent of trinkets traded by earlier explorers, the population received a few antiquated asthma-measuring devices in return for their blood. Thirty percent of Tristan da Cunha residents suffer from asthma, but, if ever an asthma therapy is developed, they will have to buy the drugs that were developed from their own blood.

There are many examples of bioprospecting like Tristan da Cunha. The people who are mined for their genetic make-up seldom see any compensation or profit medically from the research, let alone kept informed of what is being done with their blood. One woman in Papua New Guinea was surprised to learn that her cell line was being patented by the U.S. Department of Agriculture.

The philosophy behind this biopiracy and bioprospecting is one of ends justifying the means. Through genetics, it is claimed, technology will be developed that will give greater yields on crops and provide the world with cures for many of its diseases. Further, the enforcement of U.S. style intellectual property rights internationally will improve the economies and, somehow, the democratic process of developing countries. "We must extend the understanding of development and of democratic capitalism," Edmund J. Pratt, former Chairman and CEO of Pfizer Inc. explains, "helping people and governments see that improving intellectual property protection is in their enlightened self-interest. We must help them realize that the real reasons for embracing property rights are not just to comply with GATT, or to gain entry into the EU Customs Union, or to avoid U.S. trade sanctions, but to provide a base for the extension of liberal democratic principles that can lift economies and better lives."[45]

The idea that because patents created the grand technological and economical monolith that is the United States, it can also help many developing countries develop their technologies and economies is arguable. In fact, academics, industry representatives, and policy makers continue to question whether a patent system is the best vehicle for promoting a country's technology and economy. Critics of the patent system point to Japan's post-war technological progress in which, paradoxically, a lack of patent protection was key to the country's success. As we will see in Chapter six, even technological leaps in the United States came about only after patent laws were loosened, most notably within the aerospace and automobile industries.

The most recent addition to the debate comes from the Commission on Intellectual Property Rights (CIPR), a body of lawyers, economists, and scientists assigned by the British government to look at how IPRs function in developing countries. CIPR's September 2002 report found that the Western-style patent system works well in some cultural contexts and clearly stifles innovation and competition in other contexts.[46] "The central message," *The Economist* reported on the CIPR document, "is both clear and controversial: poor places should avoid committing themselves to rich-world systems of IPR protection unless such systems are beneficial to their needs."[47] The report indicates that the best that can be said is that sometimes in some contexts the patent system promotes scientific and technological advance and sometimes it does not.

Although this is not the place for an in-depth survey of the U.S. patent system and its impact on international politics, we might take a moment to look at an example—found in the context of AIDS research and drugs—in which a U.S. style patent system can actually be deadly to a developing country.

African countries suffer from a double blow from the patent system with regard to AIDS and patents: First, in the quest for life patents through bioprospecting and second, in the effect of patents on the cost and distribution of drugs and therapies.

The populations of Africa are a desirable target for

Western AIDS researchers since the disease is believed to have originated there. Researchers have conducted a number of studies on the disease in African populations, resulting in numerous patents. France's Institut Pasteur holds a patent that covers a mutant of HIV virus-1 that was isolated from an African man's blood in 1986.[48] No cures, of course, have come from this genetic research and these life patents. But the drugs and therapies that have been developed to treat AIDS are not helping Africans because of obstacles placed there in part by the international patent system.

Members of the World Trade Organization (WTO) agreed to and signed an agreement called the Trade Related International Property Rights Agreement (TRIPs) in 1994. Under the agreement, countries cannot buy or sell inventions—in this case drugs—without paying royalties to the owner of the invention. The idea is to restrict the pirating of one country's technologies by another. TRIPs was created based on U.S. patent policy, and is duly supported by biotechnology and pharmaceutical companies. "Lily...recognizes the significant contributions that U.S. trade laws and the World Trade Organization (WTO) rules have made in the area of intellectual property protection," the pharmaceutical company Eli Lilly states on its web page. "We support their continued use to encourage developing countries to provide effective patent protection for pharmaceutical products."[49]

Over four million South Africans are infected with AIDS. In the past three years, 400,000 South Africans have died of the disease. If left unchecked, 20 million Africans will soon die of the disease. Diseases that are wrecking the social, political, and economic structures of their countries can be slowed or even halted by drugs that have been successfully developed and are already on the market. But, as we know, African countries are not wealthy, nor are their people and the drugs are prohibitively expensive.

African lawmakers faced a critical decision in the late 90s:

obey international patent law and watch AIDS decimate their countries or override the TRIPs Agreement by allowing the sale of cheaper generic brands of AIDS drugs.

"Very few people understand the process of irreversible decline," Stephen Lewis, UN Special Envoy on HIV/AIDS in Africa, says. "We will have failed states. I don't think that's avoidable now."[50]

In 1997, the South African government decided to break international law and allow the sale of generic drugs.

A South African judge, himself infected with HIV, put the matter bluntly in March of 2001: "International agencies, national governments, and especially those who have the primary power to remedy the inequity—the international drug companies—have failed us in the quest for accessible treatment."[51] The South African government and other representatives from African countries felt that despite amazing research discoveries in medicine, the people most in need of medical advancements were being left behind. And the tool that was used to keep their people sick was the TRIPs agreement.

In 1997, the Clinton administration responded to South Africa's decision by threatening to use sanctions against South Africa. The U.S. has harsh penalties for countries that go against the TRIPs agreement. Under the Trade Act of 1974 and a subsequent 1988 amendments, the U.S. gives itself the right to authorize economic sanctions against any country that does not adhere to fair trade practices. Even if another country does obey international agreements like TRIPs, the U.S. can still impose penalties on it if it does not provide "fair and adequate" patent protection.[52]

Vice President Gore was continually peppered by questions on the issue while he ran for president. To avoid a political embarrassment, the Clinton administration backed down from the threat of sanctions.

Then, in the spring of 2001, thirty-nine international pharmaceutical companies, from Eli Lilly to Bayer, sued the government of South Africa for patent infringement. It was not that the drug companies thought that they were losing a large market for their drugs. Because of the expense of the drugs, South Africans had never bought many of the drug companies' products in the first place. But the companies thought that, by over-riding patent protection, the South African government was setting a bad precedent that might be taken up by other countries.

"Patents are an essential part of our business. We have to fight all attempts to erode intellectual-property rights," a spokesman for the European Pharmaceutical Industry Association said.[53]

"There was a feeling that if a country deliberately went against TRIPs, there would be a castle-of-cards effect. Without patents, the industry ceases to exist," Jean-Pierre Garnier, chief executive of GlaxoSmithKline, said.

In a letter to the South African Vice President, the European Trade Commission sided with the pharmaceutical companies and warned that if South Africa overruled drug patents they would "negatively affect the interests of the European pharmaceutical industry."[54]

"The TRIPs agreement was probably the greatest political economic achievement that the pharmaceutical industry ever had," Jim Keon, president of a trade organization that represents generic drugs (who has a vested interest in the weakening of those patent arrangements) told *The New York Times*. "Now it's coming home to roost, though. Can the world afford it? Is it ethical?"

In response to the lawsuit, thousands protested across the globe, from Cape Town to Yale University. South Africa was said to be "suffering an apartheid of drugs" under the drug companies and patent protection.[55]

"There can be no better world whilst people in developing countries are dying from curable diseases just because these drugs are so expensive," Blade Nzimande, secretary general of the South African Communist Party, said addressing protestors in Cape Town.[56]

"Here in the wealthy West, we have antiretroviral drug cocktails which prolong life, improve the quality of life, and serve, as it were, to save life," Stephen Lewis observes. "We have the drugs. We use them. In the developing world, where 95 percent of the new infections occur, virtually everyone HIV-positive is doomed to a gruesome and painful death. The numbers of people who can afford the drug cocktails are so infinitesimal as to be invisible."[57]

Under international pressure, the drug companies dropped the suit in April 2001. Further, they agreed to work with the United Nations towards making the drugs cheaper for Africans. As of January 2003, however, it is questionable whether a deal will be reached. "The negotiations are a farce," Lewis says, "they redefine the meaning of bad faith. Nothing of consequence has been agreed. It's really the monumental scandal of our times... The drugs exist and the money is available to prolong and improve the lives of millions."[58]

Even while it pressures other countries to obey TRIPs, the U.S. agrees to enforce TRIPs domestically only when it is in its best interest. When TRIPs was first proposed, Congress was worried that the WTO would take away U.S. ability to set its own regulations domestically. The Clinton administration soothed lawmakers by noting that WTO has no way of enforcing its laws.[59] If the WTO ever started pushing the U.S. around, the administration assured Congress that the U.S. would withdraw from the organization.

"U.S. influence in the WTO has more often meant U.S. domination than responsible leadership," Aileen Kwa, with the Focus on the Global South organization in Thailand, writes. "Instead of promoting beneficial goals for all, the U.S. is too often concerned with aggressively expanding its own markets."[60]

Furthermore, the U.S. and Western countries may have a lower threshold for the "emergency" exception that TRIPs provide for. Under the agreement, a country can override a patent in the face of a national emergency. Apparently, the 400,000 AIDS deaths in South Africa did not qualify as an emergency according to the drug companies. Meanwhile, across the globe, Congress and the Bush administration considered overriding a patent on an antibiotic called Cipro after 30 Americans tested positive for anthrax exposure in the fall of 2001. Canada went ahead and overrode the patent, even though no one in that country was affected and there were many other antibiotics that could battle anthrax, including penicillin. Unlike the South African case, however, pharmaceutical companies did not wage a lawsuit against Canada for its "national emergency." The U.S. threatened to override the patent as well until Bayer backed down and reduced the price of Cipro. Health and Human Services Secretary Tommy Thompson later agreed to a $95 million deal with Bayer for 100 million tablets.[61]

Internationally, the U.S. Patent system plays favorites. Those favorites are the large multinational seed and drug companies that profit from harvesting both plant life and people alike. The patent system does not protect inventors; it protects those with the the monetary capital and the legal power to create monopolies. The novelist John LeCarré researched the international pharmaceutical industry for his book *The Constant Gardener* and came away disgusted with the whole system. In a nonfiction article for *The Nation*, LeCarré condemned U.S.-style patent laws and the industries they protect:

> In the cold war, the right side lost but the wrong side won, said a Berlin wit. For the blink of a star, back there in the early nineties, something wonderful might have happened: a Marshall Plan, a generous reconciliation of old enemies, a remaking of alliances and, for the Third and Fourth Worlds, a commitment to take on the world's real enemies: starvation, plague, poverty, ecological devastation, despotism and colonialism by all its other names. But that wishful dream supposed that enlightened nations

spoke as enlightened nations, not as the hired mouth-pieces of multibillion-dollar multinational corporations that view the exploitation of the world's sick and dying as a sacred duty to their shareholders.[62]

CHAPTER THREE

Rosy Promises, Scary Predictions and Hard Realities

Genetic Tests and Gene Therapy

> Our leading scientists and scientific entrepreneurs (two labels that are increasingly interchangeable) assure us that these feats of technological prowess, though marvelous and complex, are nonetheless safe and reliable. We are told that everything is under control... The list of malfunctions gets little notice; biotechnology companies are not in the habit of publicizing studies that question the efficacy of their miraculous products or suggest the presence of a serpent in the biotech garden.
>
> —Barry Commoner
> *Harper's*, February 2002[1]

The first life patent was granted by the Supreme Court to a biochemist named Ananda Chakrabarty. Chakrabarty had developed a bacterium in his laboratory that theoretically "ate" oil spills in the ocean. The little-publicized irony of Chakrabarty's invention is that it did not work. Between 1972 when he applied for the patent and 1980 when it was finally granted, Ananda Chakrabarty himself discovered that his bacterium did not act in nature the way he had observed it to work in the laboratory. It did not eat oil in the ocean. Thus, the fateful Supreme Court decision that made patenting life forms and biological structures legal was based on an invention that simply did not work in its practical application.

The story of the famous Dolly, the world's first cloned sheep, holds a similar ending. Dolly is now dead and the company that produced her, PPL Therapeutics, makes the majority of its money by selling surgical glue that has nothing to do with cloned sheep. The $70 million that the company raised in order to create medicines from cloned sheep is now gone and the company's share price has plunged. Dolly is stuffed and in a museum.[2]

The promise of Chakrabarty's bacteria (a life form that could clean up a human-caused environmental disaster) and of PPL's cloned sheep (a life form that could produce medicine) was rather humble compared to the rosy future promised by some biotechnology rhetoric. A 1999 biotech advertisement in *The New York Times*, with an illustration of a double helix, reads: "Dreams made real... At the top of this ladder is a world without disease. Most disease is genetic. The faster scientists can sequence DNA, the faster they can pinpoint the causes of disease so cures can be developed."[3]

In his book, *Life Without Disease*, the physician William B. Schwartz suggests that "our exploding knowledge of the genetic mechanisms of disease begins to make plausible the once impossible dream of a largely disease-free existence."[4] Scientists and politicians used similar rhetoric when they sold the $3 billion government genome project to Congress and the American public, assuring us that "the best, perhaps only, way to alleviate disease was to map the entire genome."[5]

At other times, the biotechnology industry and hopeful pundits have promised that biotechnology will soon be able to cure our weight problems, our hair loss (and other perceived flaws in our physical appearance), our psychological issues, and, as was the case with Chakrabarty, our environmental problems.

But the Chakrabarty "invention" and PPL's Dolly are the first of what has become a long line of faulty, useless, and even dangerous "inventions" that have been produced in order to squeeze some financial benefits from life patents. The complex justifications and excuses as to why these products have ultimately failed can be summed up rather simply: we don't know enough.

The rosy predictions and promises of the biotech industry are analogous to other promises in history made by industries riding on the hopes of new technologies. The promise of nuclear energy is an apt analogy.

In 1954, Atomic Energy Commission chairman Lewis L. Strauss promised that nuclear energy would produce electricity "too cheap to meter."[6] Americans, and the world, were promised a clean, safe, and efficient new way of producing energy. The government would work with—and subsidize—private industry on an energy source that would wean us off of fossil fuels. President Eisenhower assured Americans, in a 1953 speech, that atomic energy would no longer be used to harm humankind, but instead be "consecrated to [mankind's] life."[7]

Despite the rosy promises, half a century later nuclear energy is now an idea that many consider too expensive and dangerous to continue to explore. Over 200,000 tons of nuclear waste lay in many of our backyards, waiting for technology to catch up and figure out a way for its disposal (or for Nevadans to finally let it be buried in *their* backyard).[8] While there are 103 operating reactors in the United States, no new nuclear reactors have been ordered since 1978, the construction of another 97 reactors has been cancelled, and 18 functioning reactors have been decommissioned.[9] According to the World Bank, "Bank lending for the energy sector requires a review of sector investments, institutions, and policies. Nuclear plants in the power sector would not be economic; they are large white elephants."[10]

Like the nuclear industry, biotechnology is in danger of becoming a failed financial and scientific endeavor. The problem that has emerged with biotechnology, as it did with nuclear power, is that products are developed before the science behind the technology is fully understood. In nuclear energy, scientists have yet to develop a technology that will successfully and safely dispose of the tons of nuclear waste being produced yearly. Likewise, biotechnology companies are racing ahead and producing products from life patents that are dangerous both to individual patients and society at large.

In May 2003, workers at a south Texas nuclear power plant discovered a leak in their reactor, but were unsure how it was caused. Consequently, the leak threatened to shut down nearly half of all the reactors in America because it was feared that there were problems with all of the reactors' initial construction and materials. A manager of the Texas plant made a comment that is reflective of the problems that have plagued the whole nuclear industry: "I think we have more questions than answers at this juncture."[11]

The manager's quote brings to mind a similar statement made offhandedly to *New Yorker* reporter Richard Preston by Craig Venter, the biotechnology entrepreneur par excellence of the early 90s: "My view of biology is 'We don't know shit.'"[12]

Another problem with nuclear energy going forward at this point in history is its rather besmirched public image. When we think of nuclear power, places like Three Mile Island and Chernobyl come to mind. The biotechnology industry is in danger of a similar image with the current products that it has rushed to produce from life patents.

There is another analogy that can be drawn between biotechnology and nuclear energy, however. Within all the promises of these two technologies, there are elements of truth. Nuclear energy does work, after all. It currently accounts for nearly 20% of the United States' electrical energy—and produces over 50% of the electricity used in New Jersey, New Hampshire, South Carolina, and Vermont.[13] Likewise, biotechnology is based on real science.[14] Understanding molecular biology is an essential part of understanding our health problems and in a few cases has led to important life-saving discoveries. Epogen is a good example of this.

There is nothing wrong with a little exaggeration when it comes to describing new technologies. We all hope for a better world, a world where people do not suffer needlessly, a world where we are able to solve our ecological messes. But when those promises so blatantly mismatch the actual outcomes, public distrust emerges and the entire future of the technology is threatened. Further, when technologies that are supposed to help humankind end up hurting or even killing people, then the industry has not only failed in public relations, it has failed ethically as well. The biotechnology industry is headed in this direction.

This chapter will look at some of the serpents in the biotech garden, specifically at genetic testing and gene therapy. Genetic testing is an appropriate place to start because the basic philosophy underlying these tests—that genes can be "read" to predict what will happen in a particular human body—is the basis for many of biotechnology industry's promises in general. If we can indeed predict physical and psychological diseases from our genes, then sooner or later we'll be able to manipulate those genes so that we won't be affected by disease. This is the hope of gene therapy. Further, if genes are predictive of our physical state, and the physical status of plants and animals, then we can bioengineer ourselves and our planet and create a flawless beautiful world, unaffected by disease (or undesirable physical appearances), drought, or environmental disasters. Ultimately, however, the promise of biotechnology is an impossible Garden of Eden.

Patenting Fear: Genetic Tests

If you could discover your risk for a second breast cancer or for ovarian cancer, would you? Chances are, you would. And that information would be invaluable in managing your health. Moreover it could provide hope. And dispel fear. Such is the promise of BRCA analysis.
—Myriad advertisement for
its breast cancer test

> The advertisement is problematic on three counts: it is manipulative, it is misleading, and it is misguiding. It is manipulative because it targets a vulnerable audience [watching a play about cancer]... misleading because it promotes a product with incomplete and at times incorrect information... [it] misguides women by suggesting that they contact the company directly about its BRCA1/2 genetic test rather than talk to their health care providers about genetic testing, their personal risk of breast cancer, and the potential usefulness of the tests.
>
> —Sara Chandros Hull and
> Kiran Prasad[15]

The average American will be in 3.7 car accidents in his or her life. In those accidents, an individual's chance of dying is .02%.[16] Now, imagine having to pay $2,500 for a company to tell you these statistics. The company that owns this knowledge assures you that it is pure science and, sure enough, it has documents full of statistics that demonstrate, apparently, that you have a 100% chance of being in 3.7 traffic accidents during the course of your life and a .02% chance of dying in a traffic accident. No matter what you do, the statistics don't change. According to these "facts," you could live in a cave and still get hit by a Mack truck 3.7 times.

What do you do with this information? Was it worth the $2,500? Do these statistics translate to what actually happens in your life? Is this information useful?

One would never pay $2,500 for traffic statistics. Although the statistics are based on accurate studies, not everyone will get into 3.7 traffic accidents and therefore not all people have a 100% chance of getting into an accident. Such information needs to be tailored for an individual situation: if you drive a taxi for a living, your chances of 3.7 accidents in your life time are higher than if you never drive and never enter an automobile. And, as everyone also knows, your .02% chance of dying is significantly affected by whether you buckle up, have airbags and other factors. These statistics may be important for developing safer roads or better traffic laws, but they are virtually meaningless when applied to an individual situation: They don't say anything about *your* particular risks.

It's unlikely that you knew the car accident statistics before reading them here. But you may have heard this statistic: one out of every eight women will develop breast cancer during her lifetime.[17] Approximately 40,800 women die of breast cancer annually.

In late 1996, genetic testing made national headlines when Myriad Genetics, Inc. began marketing a genetic test for its so-called breast cancer genes (BRCA), mutated DNA sequences that appeared to increase susceptibility to cancer. In its advertising, Myriad's proclamations were stunning: "Women with BRCA mutations have a lifetime risk of breast cancer between 56% and 87%."[18]

Suddenly the 1 in 8 chance that the average American woman has of developing breast cancer during her life jumps up to about 8 in 10 if she has one of these genetic mutations.

In the fall of 2002, Myriad developed a campaign to advertise its breast cancer genetic tests on television. With the ads, Myriad hopes that women will query their physicians about the test and, ultimately, take it. But the test, with its promise of "providing hope" and "dispelling fear" will cause more harm than good. The 8 in 10 statistic is seldom explained and very misleading. In the end, the television ads and Myriad's promotion of its breast cancer test multiplies the dangers of needless mastectomies, genetic discrimination, and the propagation of the myth that our health is inherited, rather than a mixed product of our lifestyles, our environment, and our biology.

A good place to start in unpacking Myriad's risk statistics is to ask who is included in the test population.

American Medical Association literature states that the statistics were taken from a group of high-risk women: women from families in which half of at-risk relatives were affected by breast cancer.[19] "Low-risk" women were not tested to see if they had the mutations and, if they did, what their chances might be of getting breast cancer. To reflect the accuracy that it claims the statistics inherently possess, Myriad's literature should read: "a group of high-risk women who tested positive to having BRCA mutations have been found to have a 56% to 87% lifetime risk of breast cancer."

Why is it important to note that only high-risk women were tested? Because the scary statistics that Myriad quotes change considerably when the test is opened up to a broader population, a recent study discovered.

"The risks that have been quoted are among the highest because they have been based on studies using high-risk families," Colin B. Begg of the Memorial Sloan-Kettering Cancer Center said. Begg authored a study published in the August 2002 *Journal of the National Cancer Institute* that found that since only patients whose mothers, sisters, or grandmothers had breast cancer were tested for Myriad's statistics, the numbers for the general population were skewed.[20] "The average risks are lower than what has been quoted," Begg concludes. "It is likely that the typical mutation carrier would have risks lower than that."[21]

By showing that there was considerable difference in the percentage of risk, or penetrance, between high-risk women and low-risk women, Begg's study did not merely indicate that low-risk women with the mutation had a better chance of not getting breast cancer. The study demonstrated that there were more factors involved in penetrance than simply having the BRCA mutation. Otherwise, an equal number of high-risk and low-risk women with the BRCA mutation would get breast cancer.

If the risk were attributed merely to genes, then one would predict that all women with the BRCA mutation would be at the same risk. Instead, even among high-risk women, the penetrance varies greatly.

In other words, a high risk woman—a woman who comes

from a family where women have had breast cancer—may be sharing other risk factors with her family other than a shared biology. A particular family's risk may be heightened by their geographic location (Is there a substantial amount of natural or human-made radiation in the area?), their shared diet, their shared personal habits, or their shared environment (Is there a smoker in the house?). "The evidence suggests that there's considerable variability in risk even among individuals who have the BRCA mutations," Begg says.

"If you say to everybody who comes in with the mutation that their breast cancer risk is up to 75% to 80% (based on the early studies), we know that is way too high," Kathy J. Helzisouer, an epidemiology professor and medical oncologist at Johns Hopkins University, says. "So what is the real risk (for the individual woman)? The answer is, we don't know."[22]

In fact, Begg's study found that the risk could be as low as 26% for some women with the BRCA mutations.

Myriad's test for the BRCA mutation costs $2,500. A boon to the company to be sure. But do the results provide patients with useful information? Unfortunately, whether a patient tests positive or negative for the BRCA mutations, the tests provide information that is about as useful as being sold statistics about traffic accidents. Two reasons account for its limited usefulness.

First, if the test finds that a patient *does not* have the mutation, she is still not given much reassurance. The BRCA tests identify mutations that appear to play a role in only about 5% of women with breast cancer. That is, 95% of women who have breast cancer do not have BRCA mutations. Further, less than 10% of the high-risk women who take the test have the BRCA mutations. An American Medical Association pamphlet used to educate health care providers makes it clear that "a negative test may be a true negative, or the patient may still be at high-risk of hereditary breast cancer from an as-yet unidentified gene mutation."[23] In fact, if a doctor has suggested that a patient spend $2,500 on Myriad's test, that patient is already considered high risk and will remain at-risk even if she does not have the BRCA mutations.

Second, if a patient learns from the test that she *does* have the mutation, there is still no way of discerning her individual risk. She may have a 56% to 89% risk, or she may have a risk as low as 26%. Myriad has clearly shown that there appears to be some correlation between the BRCA mutations and breast cancer and has proven it by testing a large population of at-risk women. But this does little to inform an individual—high risk or not—of her actual risks.

Whether a patient tests positive or negative for BRCA mutations, she is left with information that most women know already: as stated on the American Cancer Society home page, "all women are at risk for breast cancer, the biggest risk factors are being a woman and aging." The second risk factor: "Personal or family history of breast cancer."[24]

Money is the bottom line with genetic tests, however, and the cynical words of a reinsurer company rings true: "When it comes to determining the genetic risk profile, it matters little whether the risk is real or not; the important thing is how the danger is perceived."[25] In other words, the actual usefulness of a genetic test matters little to the company that markets it, what matters most is that the test is marketed in such a way that it sounds like we need it.

Myriad's statistics are meant to scare people into buying the test. By framing its marketing in scientific rhetoric, backed by laboratory studies, Myriad substantiates the product's effectiveness by playing on our modern faith in science and statistics to prey on people's fears. But Myriad's statistics also demonstrate how little scientists know about the so-called "breast cancer genes." Myriad's statistics may be "factual," but they shed very little light on why people get breast cancer and the environmental, lifestyle, and even genetic factors that account for a person's risk.

The BRCA tests reflect a problem with genetic testing in general: although we have some inkling that certain DNA sequences and gene mutations are associated with certain conditions, we are unsure of their specific relationships.

Moreover, we are unsure what relationship these DNA sequences have with other bodily functions. According to the American Medical Association, "The exact function of the BRCA1 gene is not known."[26] Even the names of the genes that Myriad tests, BRCA 1 and 2, or the "breast cancer genes," are misleading. The BRCA genes actually produce proteins which inhibit cancerous cells. Therefore, a mutation in a BRCA gene does not cause breast cancer. Rather, the mutation inhibits the ability of the protein to fight abnormal cell growth. Genetic science has shed some light on why the body sometimes fails to fend off breast cancer, but it is far from finding the actual cause of breast cancer.

"Without a healthy respect for the many factors that may influence penetrance," Drs. Wylie Burke and Melissa Austin of the University of Washington wrote in the *Journal of the National Cancer Institute*, "we will continue to overestimate the risk conferred by BRCA1 and BRCA2 mutations alone and, thus, miss opportunities to develop truly effective prevention strategies for women who are genetically susceptible to breast cancer that are based on a broad understanding of causative factors."[27]

The same life patents that protect a company's interest also severely limit the ability for researchers to discover why those genetic mutations happen, what their functions are, and how our molecular biology is related to environmental factors. The College of American Pathologists, in its statement against gene patents, states: "Throughout history, medicine has progressed from the discovery of basic anatomy to histology and cytology, none of which are patented, to the most recent discovery of genes. The recent trend of using gene patents to monopolize gene-based testing violates the medical communi-

ty's tradition of sharing information to bring the greatest benefit to patients."[28]

Myriad now owns the BRCA genes, but there are over 450
different mutations along the BRCA genes. In other words,
Myriad can restrict any further research on the BRCA
sequences and their mutations, decreasing the possibility of
solving any mysteries of genetically linked diseases.

The usefulness and accuracy of most genetic tests for individual patients is questionable at best. Many professional physician and clinical groups have suggested that, while the accuracy of genetic tests are being verified, the tests should be used
only for research and not for individual diagnosis.[29] In this vein,
the National Cancer Institute suggests that Myriad's risk estimates "can be useful for considering risk in large groups of people" but that "currently they cannot provide a precise cancer
risk for an individual."[30] These tests are corporate-owned products, however, and the idea is to sell as many of them as possible. In fact, genetic tests may be more profitable than finding
and selling a cure for the disease for one simple reason: more
people will want to take the test than will ever actually have the
disease.

Sword or Ploughshare: How the Tool Is Used

Good reasons exist to continue developing genetic tests.
For instance, researchers are trying to develop genetic tests that
will screen patients in order to ascertain how they will react to
certain medications. Each year, 2.2 million patients suffer
adverse reactions to medicines.[31] Genetic testing may help doctors customize medicines so that they will have minimal adverse
effects on the patient. Genetic testing may also assist pharmaceutical companies in choosing which are the best individuals
to be used for clinical testing of perspective drugs. Experts claim
that by selecting test patients through genetic screening, drug
companies will cut their drug development costs by 20%, per-

haps leading to cheaper drugs overall; one of the new promises of pharmacogenetics.[32] Finally, genetic testing can be used in research settings as scientists continue to try and understand correlations between genes, physical conditions, and an individual's lifestyle, history, and environment. Studies that examine patterns in large groups may give us clues to lifestyle and environmental risks involved in disease.

The point is not that Myriad's BRCA test will never be useful. Because life patents monopolize the genetic markers that these tests screen for, however, the advantageous uses of genetic tests will be stymied.

The American College of Medical Genetics makes clear just what the extent of this problem is. It criticizes the three ways in which gene patents have been enforced: "Monopolistic licensing that limits a given genetic test to a single laboratory, royalty-based licensing agreements with exorbitant up-front fees and per-test fees, and licensing agreements that seek proportions of reimbursement from testing services. These limit the accessibility of competitively priced genetic testing services and hinder test-specific development of national programs for quality assurance."[33]

Four hundred conditions, including sickle cell anemia, Down syndrome, and cystic fibrosis can now theoretically be screened for by genetic tests.[34] With the complete mapping of the human genome, the market may soon be flooded with many more. In essence, we are seeing whole conditions being claimed and owned privately. The monopoly that patents on genetic material provide is creating walls in the medical research community, dividing it into little fiefdoms.

Tests that Hurt: Repurcussions on the Patient

There is an important difference between risk statistics deduced from genetic tests and traffic statistics. Unlike traffic statistics, patients make serious lifestyle and health decisions based on the results of genetic tests. A minority of women who test positive on the BRCA test positive opt to have a mastectomy, a major surgery in which part of one or both breasts are removed.

"We've all been concerned about the numbers," Kathy Helzisouer says about the BRCA risk statistics. "Big decisions are being made based on the estimates of risk, so we need to keep doing research on it."[35]

A woman divorced her husband when he tested positive on a genetic test and she tested negative.[36] Another woman, who received a quick call from her physician telling her that she did *not* have a genetic mutation that exists in Huntington's disease patients, reported suffering depression, confusion, and a general identity crisis.[37] Genetic counselors report that sometimes those who test negative to genetic tests become more upset than those who test positive.

Genetic tests cause two possible adverse effects on an individual. First, the tests may have a negative effect on an individual's health, social well being, and lifestyle because of the basic confusion about the accuracy, usefulness and meaning of the tests. Second, the test may be used against the patient in the form of genetic discrimination by insurance companies, employers, and society at large.

These repercussions occur from an as-of-yet imprecise reading of risk. Again, even a genetic test that claims a high level of accuracy, such as the test for Huntington's disease, cannot definitely indicate when or if an individual will get the condition nor can it predict the degree to which an individual will be affected by the condition.

Negative repercussions to patients are consistently reported with genetic tests. "Even when a test is highly accurate and the clinical significance of the result is well understood, the outcome may do more to create anxiety for the patient than to provide reassurance," William Raub, Deputy Assistant Secretary of Science Policy under Health and Human Services, says. "This can occur when an apparently healthy individual tests positive for a genetic marker associated with a disease that may or may not develop at some future time… and for which no validated preventative intervention is available."[38]

Another frightening aspect of genetic tests is the chance that a test may simply be wrong, i.e., it gives a false positive. The quality of genetic tests remains questionable. Most genetic tests get less examination by the FDA than a gallon of milk at your grocery store. Although the FDA has the authority, it has decided not to regulate most of these tests.[39] The U.S. Department of Health and Human Services highlights the rather obvious negative effects of botched genetic tests with a number of reports. "False negative test results can mean delays in diagnosis and treatment," the HHS says in one of its reports. "False positive results can lead to follow-up testing and therapeutic interventions that are unnecessary, inappropriate and even potentially harmful."[40]

Patents on genetic material are what give companies control over these tests. Patents that provide a monopoly over genetic material work against the free market advantages of competition, one of those being that the quality of a product must be maintained in order to compete with other similar products. Therefore, the quality of genetic tests too is hurt by life patents. Life patents guarantee no competition, which, in turn, means less incentive to develop a better, more accurate test.

The most troubling aspect of genetic tests for patients, however, is the sense of inevitability that permeates their results, no matter how accurate the test. How does one weigh a positive test result with the knowledge that, for many of these conditions, science has not found a preventive or a cure? The majority of genetic tests now available only screen for conditions that are not curable. The best preventative measure for breast cancer might be a double mastectomy, but even that does not guarantee that one will be free from the disease.

Here is another place where traffic crash statistics differ from statistical risk indicated by genetic tests. All of us know the ways in which we can decrease our chances of getting into traffic accidents: we can drive defensively, we can drive slower, or we can stop driving altogether and use other modes of transportation. We can even work on traffic accidents from a technological and societal position; build safer cars, safer roads, or better traffic signals. We can implement public transportation systems or develop new, safer modes of moving people than by driving cars.

Genetic tests, however, test for conditions for which there are often no cures, let alone preventative measures. If these tests showed reliable information about impending disease, the way a test for malignancy of a tumor can indicate that action must be taken swiftly, then these issues of emotional impact of the test results would be secondary — you'd want the test. But when they show nothing more than correlations that say little if anything about the future health of the patient, the emotional impact of the test results becomes the primary, not secondary concern.

The companies that own gene patents and market genetic tests counter these concerns about potential psychological impacts by claiming that they have guidelines and training for health professionals who are responsible for talking to patients about genetic tests.

Because of the many reasons that a patient may choose to take a genetic test, however, it is impossible to standardize a counseling session that would prove helpful. Depending on the patient's ethnic, religious, and socioeconomic background, his or her reaction to the test results could be very different. Test results will also have a significant and sometimes unpredictable impact on the patient's loved ones and family. On top of that, in most cases physicians are given the responsibility of counseling before and after genetic tests but physician visits, as we know, are getting shorter and shorter.

There is also the question of the education and knowledge of the person giving the test or the counseling. Most genetic tests and genetic counseling is now given by primary care physicians, but gene patents actually restrict the training of doctors on genetic testing. The American College of Medical Genetics writes in its position statement against gene patents: "[Restricting the availability of gene testing through gene patents] affects the training of the next generation of medical and laboratory geneticists, physicians, and scientists in the area enveloped by the patent or license."[41]

Already there are examples of the medical community not understanding the subtleties of genetic testing or not properly explaining it to their patients, to the point where it has become dangerous. Once seldom given, pre-natal tests screening for cystic fibrosis has become more and more common in the past two years. The genetic test screens for 30 genetic mutations that have been identified as correlating to the disease. One of these mutations, labeled 5T, "is present in about five percent of the population," the magazine GeneWatch reports, "but can only lead to cystic fibrosis if a rare mutation called R117H is present."

Despite the fact that it is impossible to have cystic fibrosis with only the 5T mutation, the American College of Medical Genetics reports that 20 pregnancies have been terminated when patients learned that 5T existed alone. The Council for Responsible Genetics views the 5T issue as "a tragic lesson in what happens when the medical community's understanding of genetic information fails to keep pace with its availability."[42]

Medical professionals may soon lose control of genetic counseling altogether. The information age has created a whole world of new marketing avenues for medical products, including over 17,000 health care web sites on the internet.[43] Some of these sites are already being used to fill drug prescriptions, often with "on-line doctors" employed by the web sites who will give you the prescription and the dose in the same "visit." The ease with which drugs can be purchased over the internet can be demonstrated by the fact that a large portion of Viagra's six million plus prescriptions have been made and sent over the internet, without doctor and patient ever meeting face to face. It may not be too far in the future when genetic testing will be available over the internet and a quick "on-line counselor" will take care of the individual's psychological conditions.[44]

The point isn't that tests that don't require a doctor are bad. For example, the advent of the pregnancy test that can be administered in the privacy of one's own home was a step forward in giving people greater control over their lives. But when the results of genetic tests are so widely open to interpretation in contrast to the "you're either pregnant or you're not" result, placing these in the hands of consumers may empower drug companies financially, but they probably won't result in better health for the test taker.

The widespread use of the internet also plays a role in a second and much more frightening effect of genetic testing on the patient: discrimination. Information is collected on people who use these health care sites—twenty-five million Americans in 1999—for the most part without their knowledge or consent. Although most of these web sites have privacy policies, a recent American Association for the Advancement of Science study found that there are instances when personal data is transferred to third parties in violation of these policies. Moreover, many sites do not have sufficient security against a "casual hacker or someone actively seeking to access company databases."[45]

This means that you have only to visit a web site in order to be "tagged" and labeled as a consumer of the product sold on the site. Even if you never order a genetic test, there may be a record that you once considered it.

These general internet privacy issues are widely known and the subject of great debate. But who would want to know that you are considering a genetic test?

For Your Eyes Only? Genetic Tests and Discrimination

> Genetic discrimination is very real. People are losing their jobs because of genetic discrimination.
> —Edward McCabe, Chairman of the
> Department of Health and Human
> Services Secretary's Advisory
> Committee on Genetic Testing[46]

Let us return to the traffic accident statistic. Although those statistics may seem useless to most individuals, they are useful to insurance companies. By looking at the kind of person who has a statistical probability of being in a car accident, insurance companies set their rates and even decide whom to insure. This is why there are different rates depending on your age, your gender, and where you live. Insurance companies take statistics and use them to evaluate how much of a financial risk you may pose and calculate how to make the greatest profit.

And so it becomes clear why insurance companies might want to find out the results of a genetic test. Donna E. Shalala, former Secretary of the Department of Health and Human Services, told Congress as early as 1997 that "over 20 percent of people in families with a genetic disorder report that they, or a family member, have been refused health insurance on the basis of their genetic profile." Shalala's department also documented a number of cases where people had lost jobs or promotions, or had been turned down for adoption because of genetic information.[47] Although individual state governments have come up with varying legislation to protect individuals from genetic discrimination, most of these laws have not been tested in court.

Taking a genetic test in the privacy of your physician's office does not guarantee that the insurance company won't have access to the results. You may not even realize that you are being tested.[48] Only 45% of genetic test labs require informed consent from the patient. You may be tested during a doctor'svisit without your knowledge or permission.

Many organizations, including The National Cancer Institute, have very specific warnings about the serious implications of including genetic test results in a patient's medical records.[49] Implications for an individual include the inability to obtain new health insurance, an increase in premium payments, or the decrease in the amount or type of coverage.

Keep in mind that an individual does not actually have to have the condition—say, breast cancer—being tested for. As we have seen, it is unclear, really, what these tests are testing for. Genetic testing puts a powerful twist on the old joke: "Nothing was wrong with me until I went to the doctor." Even if the person is never actually affected by the condition, the insurance companies may treat them as if he or she already has it.

The Council for Responsible Genetics, in its position paper on genetic discrimination, outlines the risk of this kind of thinking: "Many of these people (who test positive on a genetic test) will never have a related illness, or will experience a lifetime of the asympomatic, presymptomatic or minimally symptomatic phases of the condition... Genetic testing is not only a medical procedure. It is also a way of creating social categories."[50]

The Disability Critique

Social discrimination is already evident in the administering of neo-natal genetic tests, some of which are routine for expectant mothers in the U.S. The "disability critique," articulated by disabled individuals who are pro-choice, calls attention to the "stereotypes about life with disability and about what it means to be the parent of a child who is disabled:"[51]

> As the ease of testing increases, so does the perception within both the medical and broader communities that prenatal testing is a logical extension of good prenatal care: the idea is that prenatal testing helps prospective

parents have healthy babies... If one thinks for even a
moment about the history of our society's treatment of
people with disabilities, it is not difficult to appreciate why
people identified with the disability rights movement
might regard such testing as dangerous. For the members
of this movement... living with disabling traits need not be
detrimental either to an individuals prospects of leading a
worthwhile life, or to the families in which they grow up,
or to society at large.[52]

In essence, the critique stipulates that deciding the fate of
a fetus by means of routine genetic tests is the first slip down the
slope of eugenics toward a goal of dubious "perfection." Health
professionals and insurance companies are taking away the idea
of choice if they predict "the probable genetic make-up"—
together with the cost of insurance and medical and societal
"costs" to caring for a disabled child—as a reason to abort a
fetus.

Prenatal genetic tests look at the fetus as a machine made
of genetic parts. If some of those parts are considered "faulty,"
the fetus may be considered a burden to its family or to society.
We have only to look to the last 100 years of human history—
Nazi Germany, ethnic cleansing in the Balkans, eugenic laws in
China—for evidence of the dangers encountered when a society decides that one type of person is a "burden to society" or
"less than human."

It's easy to believe that such specters would not appear in
the U.S. in an age where diversity is trumpeted, where teams of
astronauts are both ethnically and internationally diverse,
where a Republican president owes his career in no small part
to his courting of Hispanic voters and his ability to speak
Spanish. Yet the drive toward genetic discrimination may have
more insidious and effective forces behind it than we feel comfortable admitting. The power of some corporations seeking to
limit risk (in the form of health insurance companies) and other
corporations seeking cash in on products they claim can predict

that risk (biotech companies) may become an unstoppable force behind a new eugenics.

As with prenatal tests, the benefits of genetic tests that screen for incurable conditions are often evaluated in economic terms, instead of in terms of benefits for the individuals being screened for. At a recent international conference on genetic testing set up by the Organization for Economic Co-operation and Development (OECD), the risks and benefits of the genetic tests were addressed. Victor R. Grann, at the Cancer Center at Columbia University, presented a study that concluded that, in order for genetic testing for breast cancer to be cost effective, "women tested needed to be willing to have prophylactic surgery if they test positive."[53] The author weighed the total cost (to patient, hospital, and insurer) of treating breast cancer against the total cost of widespread use of the test. He found that in order for widespread testing to be cost effective, a person must agree before she even takes the test, that if the test shows she has the mutation she must undergo a mastectomy *regardless of whether she has breast cancer or not*. In the name of saving money, a mastectomy is recommended even if the risk is, as we have seen, only 26%.

It is as if it were discovered that a certain car model had a steering wheel that sometimes malfunctioned, say, in 1 in 10 cars. Because the cost to the car company, the health and insurance industries, and society at large would be too great to leave all the cars on the road, the car company calls back all the cars and, regardless of whether they actually have the malfunctioning steering wheel, remove and replace all the steering wheels. That might actually be sound policy toward a machine. But not for people. Like the car, the person is considered a group of functioning parts. Like that car, in order for the person to be "made" more economical for the health and insurance industry and society at large, both her breasts must be removed regardless of whether she is healthy or not.

The idea of assigning a monetary cost to a supposed risk

and then trying to eliminate that risk through interventions such as pre-emptive abortions or pre-emptive mastectomies is more horrifying when we understand that it is based on such a shaky, inaccurate science. It is true that the medical industry has always had to deal with weighing costs with outcomes. It must always weigh the choices that are involved in spreading their money and resources to help the most people possible, sometimes at the cost of a few. But with genetic testing, we now have a way of putting a value on individuals with genetic tests that are based on a questionable combination of statistics and marketing.

The 1998 movie *Gattaca* graphically presents the chilling valuation of the human being in a society obsessed with fallible genetic tests. An early scene depicts a hospital room immediately after the birth of the protagonist, Vincent. A nurse takes a drop of blood from the infant and, within seconds, runs a series of genetic tests on him. She reads the results to Vincent's mother: "Neurological condition: 60% probability; manic depression: 40% probability; attention deficit disorder: 89% probability; heart disorder: 99% probability..." For the rest of the story, then, Vincent is considered a part of a genetic underclass despite the fact that he never suffers from the predicted conditions and he is an intellectual genius. In his world, the actual health of the individual is ignored, job interviews are conducted and concluded through urine samples, and romantic relationships are decided by matching genetic codes.[54]

Genetic testing is still in its infancy. By patenting genes and pieces of genes that are the basis for these tests, and by having corporations exploit these tests for profit in the service of investors, we have put in place a system that severely limits any scientific good that may ultimately come from these tests. Companies are using their patents to restrict broader testing that may assist us in finding the actual causes of disease. Instead of a world without disease, life patents are being used to set up new social categories, with new methods of discrimination.

God Bless Our Genes (and Other Multifactors)

> The collapse of the doctrine of one gene for one protein, and one direction of causal flow from basic codes to elaborate totality, marks the failure of reductionism for the complex system that we call biology...
>
> —Stephen Jay Gould on
> the results of the Human
> Genome Project[55]

> reductionism. noun. the practice of simplifying a complex idea, issue, condition, or the like, esp. to the point of minimizing, obscuring, or distorting it.
>
> —Webster's Unabridged
> Dictionary of the English
> Language

"It's in my genes."

"It must be genetic."

"Look at his gene pool."

These phrases roll off our tongues as easily as saying "God bless you" when someone sneezes. Like "God bless you," we seldom reflect on the meaning of a phrase like "it's in my genes." What does "God bless you" mean when we say it after someone sneezes? In fact, the word "bless" comes from an Old English word that means "to redden with blood" and which later came to mean "to consecrate." So "God bless you" actually means "God bathe you in blood" or "God consecrate you."[56]

In the same manner, when we say "it's in the genes" to describe an ability or talent we have (or, more likely, a psychological habit or physical trait that we don't really like), we do not stop and consider the actual biological processes that we are crediting or blaming.

"God bless you" comes from a time in history when most if not all of the people you heard sneeze were Christian, or at least believed in a God. In its time, it made perfect sense to ask a mutually shared God to look after a neighbor's health, believing that a God controlled whether our neighbor was healthy or sick. It makes less sense now, as not all people we now meet share the same God and many do not believe in any God. A great many people that we say "God bless you" to probably do not believe God has anything to do with a sneeze whether they believe in a deity or not. Still, we use the phrase, perhaps simply to mean "may you stay in good health, through whatever means."

Likewise, phrases like "it's in the genes" come from an idea espoused not so long ago in which many of our physical and psychological traits were thought to come from tiny entities in our bodies called genes. The theory was that there were hundreds of thousands of these little entities, each of which programmed a protein to do a specific job in our bodies. Associated with this theory was the idea that many of our diseases were caused because these genes were not doing their job.

That theory has been annihilated by scientists in recent studies. The most surprising news to come out of the government's Human Genome Project was the fact that humans have only about 35,000 genes. This conclusion confirmed the work of many scientists who were discovering that our molecular biology was much more complicated than once believed.

So what is a gene? And how does it affect our physical and psychological status?

Before the human genome project, the basic definition for a gene was a DNA sequence that encoded proteins. That is, a gene supposedly gave a "message" to a protein to carry out a function within the human cell. We now know that most DNA sequences may encode many different proteins, each with a different message. Nor is the DNA-to-protein message a one-way street. Enzymes can translate a message from RNA into DNA. "We need to think of DNA, RNA, and proteins as all acting upon one another, rather than assuming a neat line from DNA to protein," Harvard geneticist Ruth Hubbard and writer Elijah Wald write in their book *Exploding the Gene Myth*.[57]

Many scientists question whether the term "gene," which implies a single, definable, self-sustaining system, is too antiquated a concept to use in current genetic research. MIT professor Evelyn Fox Keller reflects:

> Sequence information has led to the identification of repeated genes, split genes, overlapping genes, cryptic DNA, anti-sense transcription, nested genes, transposition, multiple promoters that allow for alternative sites of and variable criteria for the initiation of transcription—all of which have hopelessly confounded hope for a structural definition of the gene.[58]

What is no longer considered truth is the reductionist concept that one gene codes one protein to do a job. The relationship between our genotype (our genetic characteristics) and our phenotype (our physical characteristics, including health conditions) is also hopelessly confounded.

It is true that mutations in some genes correlate directly to a small number of human diseases. The discovery of "single gene disorders" or monogenetic diseases fuelled the myth that one gene coded one protein and therefore our diseases could be traced to mutations within a single gene. Genetic tests that screen single gene disorders such as Huntington's disease and hemoglobin diseases indeed give much higher risk statistics than tests such as the BRCA test.

But monogenetic diseases are the exception, not the rule. Monogenetic diseases, in fact, are quite rare. Samuel Wilson, deputy department head of the National Institute of Environmental Health Science, puts it this way: "Pure, genetically caused disease represents five to 10 percent of the disease burden in the United States; the rest is lined to a combination of multiple factors, both genetic and environmental."[59]

The rest of our diseases, including the most common such as cancer, heart disease, and diabetes, are called multifactoral; i.e., they are caused by a multitude of factors.

Even tests for monogenetic diseases cannot predict how a certain condition will affect an individual patient. "At the moment we cannot predict for certain the clinical course of any simple monogenetic disease," David J. Weatherall concluded in a study published in the *British Medical Journal.* "The idea that we may be able to predict the occurrence of a heart attack or the onset of diabetes from examining a child's genotype at birth is even further away. Even for the monogenetic diseases we still do not know what is just "noise" in the system and what is clinically important."[60]

Just as we now know that there are more elements to our health than merely spiritual (Gesundheit!), we now also know that there are more elements to our health than the now rather antiquated idea of "genes."

At the same time the government's genome project announced it had finished mapping the human genome, the most comprehensive cancer study ever conducted released its results.[61] The study, conducted in Scandinavia on 90,000 human twins, received very little press, especially compared to the fanfare that surrounded the genome project's announcement. While the genome project grandly announced that its discoveries would help researchers find genetic causes for diseases, the twins study humbly suggested that we have barely looked at the other areas that are most responsible for our diseases.

The twins cancer study concluded that "inherited genetic factors make a minor contribution to susceptibility to most types of neoplasm. This finding indicates that the environment has the principal role in causing sporadic cancer." Paul Lichtenstein, the lead researcher on the study, told *The Washington Post,* "Environmental factors are more important than genetic factors, and that's important to remember, especially since everyone thinks that everything is solved now that we have the human genome in our computers."[62]

Hundreds of studies on a small, round worm named

Caenorhabditis elegans give us more proof that the idea that our physical and psychological conditions are genetically-based is reductionist to the point of being misleading.

C. elegans is such a popular creature—it was the October 1995 *Science* magazine coverworm and centerfold[63]—it is currently being studied by approximately 1,000 researchers worldwide.[64] C. elegans is not a complex creature, but it is popular because 40% of its genes are similar to those of other organisms. C. elegans contributes to our discussion on genetically-based diseases because of one striking fact: of the hundreds, perhaps thousands, of genetic studies that C. elegans has been through, none of the research on it has yielded a pure connection between a single gene and a single behavior.[65]

Using C. elegans as an example, Kenneth F. Schaffner, a professor of Medical Humanities at George Washington University, outlines eight different rules that should be considered when research tries to connect a gene or DNA sequence with a particular behavior or condition.[66] Environmental impact is, of course, one of the considerations, but others include the changing nature of gene expressions (they seem to learn, even in simple organisms like C. elegans) and the complexity of relationships between different genes, proteins, and other molecular matter that we seldom hear anything about.

The focus on genes as the primary focus of disease also relieves society of the responsibility of dealing with disease that is caused by human factors. Biotechnology concentrates on biological causation of diseases, instead of analyzing suffering as a problem that stems from human's treatment of each other, the most obvious examples of which can be found in violence, oppression, and prejudice. Though many of the diseases that currently plague the majority of the world are directly caused by social and political problems such as poverty, sanitation, proper shelter, and basic medical care, a disproportionate amount of financial and medical resources are being put into genetic research.

"(I)f all of people's health and behavior are functions of their genes, then we can blame social ills on the inadequacies of individuals," Ruth Hubbard and Elijah Wald write, "not on economic and other societal problems."[67]

While biotech advertisements announce that genetic research will soon produce "a world without suffering,"[67] 12.2 million children die every year because they haven't received treatments that already exist, many costing under a quarter.[69]

Much of our recent research on disease has been on genes, however, and their effect on our health. Thus, the claiming of genes as hot properties with life patents. This focus is probably detrimental not only to finding the real causes of disease, but also to reaching conclusions that have scientific validity. "Failure to collect data on environmental factors that may modify the relation between genotype and disease can also lead to inconsistency and confusion," Harvard epidemiologist Walter C. Willett reported in *Science*. He concludes:

> Overly enthusiastic expectations regarding the benefits of genetic research for disease prevention have the potential to distort research priorities and spending for health. However, the integration of new genetic information into epidemiologic studies can help clarify causal relations between both life-style and genetic factors and risks of disease. Thus, a balanced approach should provide the best data to make informed choices about the most effective means to prevent disease.[70]

The amazing progress in fighting lung cancer is a good example of studying and preventing disease at the lifestyle or environmental level. Lung cancer research has developed little in the way of miraculous new drugs or cures, but it has pointed out things we can do to prevent lung cancer in the first place, i.e., stop smoking and pass laws that will cut down on our contact with second hand smoke. The research on smoking concentrated on how our biology reacted to environmental factors and lifestyles to cause a disease.

This is again why monopolies over specific genetic structures stand in the way of real progress in finding out the causes of many of our health problems. If only one organization is allowed to research a certain gene—and goes in the direction of marketing genetic tests from their research instead of looking for actual causes—then the patent system is being used to hold back lifesaving research.

The materials in our homes, buildings and roads, the pollution in our air, the chemicals in our food, water, and household products, and, ironically, modern technological "achievements" such as genetically engineered food may all have negative impacts on our health. Most of these remain woefully under-examined. In some cases, we don't have the technology or the information needed to research these areas. Or, as was the case with cigarettes, many believe the scientists who are paid by the industries that stand to lose the most from examining these areas of disease prevention.

Because our molecular biology is so much more complex than we once thought—and it is affected by so many unpredictable environmental factors—simply tinkering with our genes is not going to bring about a world without disease. A Garden of Eden brought about by biotechnology—is simply not possible. Reengineering our molecular biology will not solve all our problems.

Lives vs. Profit Margins: Gene Therapy

> Looking back, I can see that I was fairly naïve to have been as trusting as I was.
>
> —Paul Gelsinger, whose son Jesse died as result of an experiment in gene therapy.[71]

Four days after beginning human trials on gene therapy in

September 1999, eighteen-year-old Jesse Gelsinger died, making him the first known death caused by a gene therapy experiment.[72] Gene therapy—the transfer of normal or redesigned cells into a patient in order to reduce or alleviate a diseased state—was one of the original products promised by biotechnology companies. Researchers, however, have yet to develop any successful gene therapies.

The lead researcher in Jesse's experiment, Dr. James Wilson, was also founder of Genovo Inc., a company that helped fund the University of Pennsylvania's Institute for Human Gene Therapy, which conducted the experiment. Genovo was later sold to a larger company and Dr. Wilson took home $13.5 million in stocks.[73]

Medical accidents take place all the time, and it may seem unfair to point to Gelsinger's death as an indicator of corporate greed racing to cash in on the patent wars. But after Jesse Gelsinger died, the National Institutes of Health discovered that, since 1977, six other deaths had occurred in gene therapy experiments.[74] Worse, the researchers in those experiments had consciously kept the details of the deaths hidden from both the NIH and the public. The Gelsinger case set off a series of debates and public forums on experimenting with human subjects and the usefulness of genetic therapy.

"As a nation we can do a better job of protecting the human subjects in gene-therapy studies than we have done during the past ten years," the director of the Kennedy Institute of Ethics at Georgetown University told a Congressional subcommittee after the incident. "The death of a generous young man, the serious side effects experienced by several and perhaps numerous other subjects, and the almost-total breakdown of the system for reporting serious adverse events... should be a wake-up call to us all."[75]

The NIH found serious problems with the oversight policies of the organizations conducting the human gene therapy experiments. Much of the responsibility of overseeing these human experiments falls on institutional review boards or IRBs. Hospitals, universities, or companies traditionally set up IRBs to review the human experiments conducted by their respective organizations. The boards are established to make sure that ethical and medical concerns in human experiments are continually addressed.

Recently, however, hospitals and research institutions have begun to contract out this responsibility. That is, they pay an outside private entity to act as their IRB. This means that research institutions hire a for-profit board to review their research to make sure that human subjects are not exposed to unreasonable risks.

In June 1998, the Office of the Inspector General in the U.S. Department of Health and Human Services issued a report warning that many IRBs may be ineffective.[76] They documented a number of conflicts of interests that cloud the mission of the IRBs.

Imagine you are a researcher, excitedly pursuing a fast-track miracle genetic drug. You need to get human trials going right away, so that you will be able to prove that this genetic drug works on humans to, say, cure some form of cancer. You hope this drug will not only benefit humankind, of course, but will net you and the pharmaceutical company that is backing you a billion-dollar corner on the "curing cancer market." Will you submit your proposed research to the slow, bureaucratic, local hospital IRB for consideration, knowing it may question some of what you intend to do to the human subjects? Or will you pay your money and get a quick turn around time from a for-profit IRB?

Now imagine you are the for-profit IRB. Are you going to tell your paying client that she or he cannot do the experiments? If you do, will that client ever hire you again? If you find problems with the treatment of the human subjects, what will your reputation be among other researchers who are looking for the go-ahead on their experiments?

The conflict of interest is obvious on at least two levels: One, there is a danger that the researchers working on experiments with human subjects may be driven more by profit or blind faith in their own research. They may not make decisions in the best interest of the human subjects and will choose IRBs who will agree with them instead of IRBs that will truly have the patients' well being in mind. Two, private IRBs are of necessity driven by profits and, like any other business, will seek to make the researchers happy. "The customer is always right" may have frightening repercussions. When the entity that is being regulated is the same as the customer—watch out!

The number of for-profit IRBs has increased dramatically in the past few years, and their business is steadily growing.[77] Their customers include research institutes and hospitals, many of which use federal money to fund their experiments.

Even nonprofit IRBs that are housed within institutions such as universities may have conflicts of interest. In May 1999, the U.S. government shut down human experiments at Duke University because the government found that Duke's IRB was not adequately protecting human patients.[78] The IRB did not keep track of the human studies after they had begun and had failed to document special, federally mandated protections for children. On some of its votes, Duke's IRB may not have had a quorum present. Specifically, the government found that a voting member of the IRB was also in charge of obtaining Duke's grants and contracts. In other words, a person in charge of making the university look good to pharmaceutical and biotechnology companies was also put in charge of the safety of the participants.

Research, even outside of a private corporation, can very rarely be "not for profit." Ever since the passage of the Bayh-Dole Act in 1980, the majority of research is funded with a combination of public and private money. IRBs must balance protection of human subjects with the fact that their institutions are being paid to produce results.

"We did not foresee the emergence of venture capital... and researchers who invest in and oversell the promise [of their research] and keep adverse effects quiet," says Maxine Singer, a molecular biologist who worked with the NIH in the 1970s. "While this creates exciting and constructive competition, some scientists have compromised their behavior."[79]

Most gene therapy experiments currently do not use patentable material, but the eventual hope is that successful processes or biological materials for gene therapy will be patented. For instance, patents may be sought on genetically altered viruses that would deliver genes to a specific part of the body.

But the drive to make a profit from a life patent can lead to an ethically blind race for a product. Patent-owning biotech companies that must show results to stockholders, pharmaceutical companies that need to recoup exorbitant research costs, and genetic researchers driven by scientific zeal and hubris all combine together to make up a dangerous mix. They are driven, sometimes at the cost of human lives, to make money from their life patents.

Safety Saves Industry

As we will see in Chapter Five, the aerospace industry needed government regulation in order to insure that the public saw airplanes as a safe technology. Although the phrase, "government regulations," sends a chill down any businessman's spine, the biotechnology industry itself requires regulation in order for it to survive. Part of the problem with jump-starting the aerospace industry was the fact that the general public viewed the early airplanes as extremely dangerous. The average person could not imagine that the mechanical deathtraps would be useful to anyone save pilot daredevils at circuses and fairs. In a more modern example, part of the negative reputation of nuclear energy is the idea that it is unsafe.

Similarly, experiments in genetic tests, genetic databases,

and genetic therapy are quickly getting a reputation for being based on faulty science. "Already in genetics research studies, we are seeing individuals who opt not to participate in research because of their fear that this information could fall into the wrong hands," Francis Collins, director of the National Human Genome Research Institute, told *The Scientist*.[80] Test subjects are not being told how their DNA will ultimately be used, culminating in widespread doubt in genetic databases. twenty thousand Icelanders opted out of the deCode database because they disagreed with how the information would be used or felt like their consent had been ignored. Other test subjects are driven to use lawsuits to reclaim the scientific use of their DNA, such as the families affected by Canavan disease that sued Miami Children's Hospital. Gene therapy makes more headlines about mistakes and conflicts of interest than it does on successful medical treatment.

There is a lack of public confidence in medical trials on humans in general. A 2002 Harris Interactive survey found that the majority of people surveyed were only "somewhat confident" that patients will be treated well in trials and only a quarter were very confident that "new treatments are tested on humans only after there is valid scientific evidence that the treatments are likely to be effective and safe." Ironically, the article in *Health Care News* published by Harris Interactive concluded that a solution would be a marketing campaign to increase people's confidence in medical trials.[81]

The patenting of genes and genomes may be just the beginning in a long line of life patents and monopolies on other biological molecules. Already, the biotechnology industry's rhetoric has moved from genomics to the area of proteomics, the study of molecular proteins. "In terms of research, genomics is passé and proteomics is the new buzz work," faculty Dean of Harvard Medical School Joseph D. Martin said. Harvard is seeking $100 million in private and public funds to study proteins.[82] Where once the exploration of our genes promised to give us enough information to develop a plethora of disease fighting drugs and therapies, now biotechnology is trumpeting proteins. The so-called proteomic revolution has many of the same promises that the genomic revolution proclaimed. "Knowing the structure of the protein gives you a big clue in how to build drugs," says John Novell, head of the NIH's proteomics effort.[83] Companies that once mapped the human genome are now looking to map out all human proteins. But their research will lack public support—and financial support— if the today's biotechnology "products" are allowed to run rampant over people's health and human rights.[84]

A new marketing campaign is not what is needed in order to gain public support for the biotechnology industry.[85] Nor does the general public merely need to be "better educated" about the science and the research as many scientists and businessmen seem to condescendingly imply. Perhaps instead, the scientists and businessmen need to be regulated much more closely.

The Patent Office is a good place to start with a little more Congressional and public oversight. At the very least we should be watching a little more closely what the Patent Office is doing and has been doing for the past two decades. In the next chapter, we will take a close look at some of the convoluted reasoning of the Patent Office that has allowed the patenting of life.

CHAPTER FOUR

Of Mice and Mousetraps

The Patent Office Requirements

> We believe that composition of matter patents should not be issued for any DNA, particularly human DNA, nor for any related cDNA, EST or other nucleotide sequences, because such compounds exist in nature, have been identified and placed in public domain for over 15 years, or otherwise are obvious to derive in light of the current technology.
>
> —MJ Research, a Massachusetts biotechnology firm, in a letter to the U.S. Patent Office.[1]

One of the key tenets of the United States 210-year-old patent system is that it's technology neutral," the former director of the Patent Office, Todd Dickinson, explained to a Congressional subcommittee. "From gear shifts to genomics, it applies the same norms to all inventions and technologies... Just as the patent system has nurtured the development of telephony, aeronautics, and computers, so, too, will it ensure that the new discoveries in genomics lead to healthier, longer lives for all humankind."[2]

Indeed, when we think of patents, we think of the honor that is bestowed upon the brilliant men and women in history who have bettered society through their inventions. The idea of patenting brings to mind the great scientific inventions that changed the way we live: the steam engine, the telegraph and the telephone. We think of patents as awards of recognition for men and women who spent their lifetimes figuring out solutions to the problems of everyday life—how to get from here to there, how to cure illnesses, how to live healthier, and how to communicate better with each other. These are scientists who have studied the laws of nature and made them work for us.

But the patent system's tenet of being technology neutral does not work in the case of molecular biology and plants and animals. The patent system's unchanging requirements fail when one tries to force such things as the so-called "breast cancer gene" and Bolivian quinoa into the same definitions of inventions as airplanes and telephones.

In this chapter, we will look at the three elements required by the U.S. Patent and Trademark Office in order for an "invention" to be awarded a patent. Let us say I want to patent a wooden mousetrap. I must prove three things in my application to the Patent Office:

It must be novel (new). I will win a patent on my mousetrap if I prove that no one has invented one like it. Previous inventors may have used wood to create other kinds of mousetraps, so my mousetrap must demonstrate that it is using these elements in a way that others have not considered.

It must not be obvious. A customary use of a natural object cannot be patented.[3] That is, though my mousetrap uses naturally occurring material like wood, I am using that wood in a completely new and non-obvious way to make my mousetrap. My invention must be more "inventive" than a simple piece of wood you might find in the forest, since a piece of wood that you can use to kill a mouse is too "obvious" to be considered an invention.

It must have credible, specific and substantial utility. I have to prove that my wood actually does something, i.e., catches mice. The idea of utility is the difference between an invention (wood that does something) and art (wood that does nothing).

So, my application for the patent must clearly outline how

my mousetrap meets these requirements. The Patent Office would then decide if my invention meets the requirements: Is it novel or new? Yes. It is made from wood but in a way never before thought of. Is it non-obvious? Yes. No one looking at a piece of wood would think of using it in this way. Does it have utility or function? Yes. At least theoretically, the mousetrap can catch mice.

My mousetrap must fulfill all three of these requirements. It is not enough that I invent some new and non-obvious contraption, it must also actually do something (utility) in order to be patentable. Likewise, I cannot simply present something useful without also proving that it is not similar to an already invented contraption (novel).

Given these requirements, the question presents itself: How can things found in our bodies and in nature—like the BRCA genes, wild rice, and *Mycobaceterium tuberculosis*—be considered "inventions" by biotech companies and by the Patent Office?

This chapter will start with some of the patents that have been discussed in the previous chapters in light of Patent Office requirements, including patents on genes, on genomes, and on the molecular biology of plants already found in nature. These patents seem to clash with a basic Patent Office tenet that things found in nature are not patentable. Then we will examine other genetic "inventions," such as genetically modified plants and animals. With these genetic inventions, there appears to be at least a modicum of "inventiveness," i.e. there is a difference between what is found in nature and what has been invented. These inventions deserve special analysis with regard to Patent Office requirements.

By now it should be clear that there is a wide range of patents on life, from clear rip-offs of naturally-occurring wild rice to genetically modified mice, from patents on small snippets of uncharacterized DNA to patents on whole cows. Some of these fulfill some of the Patent Office requirements some of the time and, more importantly, appear to serve a public good. For example, a life patent owned by Amgen on a protein called EPO has credible utility and real world use. In fact, as we will see later in the chapter, EPO has been used to save lives.

With all of these life patents, however, there are two questions that keep arising: First, should we grant proprietary rights over DNA, plants, animals, and other things found in nature in the first place? Second, if we feel there should be some proprietary protection for some of these so-called inventions—say, for bioengineered mice, do we want to leave it up to the Patent Office to make the decisions on how broad that ownership should be, especially given the consequences?

The "Novelty" of Life Patents

The key to understanding the Patent Office's justification for life patents lies in how humans have altered things found in nature. As Gary Walsh, a biochemist at the University of Limerick, explains, "patenting is possible if the 'hand of man' has played an obvious part in developing the product."[4]

The U.S. Supreme Court initially raised the starter gun for the race on life patents in the 1980 decision, *Diamond v. Chakrabarty*. In that case, the majority of the court allowed a company to patent bacteria that "ate" oil spills on the ocean surface. Bacteria, by most people's definitions, are living things found in nature, but Ananda Chakrabarty's "invention" was a microorganism that he created in the laboratory by combining plasmids from different bacteria.[5] At first, the Patent Office refused to grant Chakrabarty a patent, explaining that a microorganism is a "product of nature" and therefore can not be patented. The Supreme Court overturned this ruling, stating that the microorganism was "not nature's handiwork, but [Chakrabarty's] own; accordingly it is patentable subject matter."

The Supreme Court was closely divided on the *Chakrabarty* decision, 5-4. The dissenting opinion warned of the consequences of allowing patents on living things, genetically modified or not.

Using the *Chakrabarty* decision as its justification, the Patent Office now allows all genetically modified organisms (GMOs)—plants, animals, or microorganisms that are genetically altered, added to, or modified—to be patentable because, theoretically, the "hand of man" created a new organism.[6] We will look more closely at GMOs later in this chapter and how they fit into the Patent Office's requirement. Leaving GMOs aside for a moment, however, how did the Patent Office move from allowing GMOs to be patented—arguably novel human inventions—to allowing pathogens, genes within our bodies, and plants found in the mountains of South America to be patented?

Again, the "hand of man" rationale is used. Patents on genes are considered "invented" and patentable because the patented DNA has been isolated and purified.

"It might be argued that simply to find any substance naturally occurring on the earth is categorized as a discovery, and would be unpatentable because it lacks true novelty or any inventive step," Walsh explains. "However, if you enrich, purify, or modify a product of nature such that you make available for the first time in an industrially useful format, that product/process is generally patentable…. In the USA, purity alone often facilitates patenting of a product of nature."

The distinction between "purified" forms of DNA and "native" DNA found in life forms was first made in the Federal Circuit case, *Amgen Inc. v Chugai Pharmaceutical Company* in 1991, almost as an afterthought.[7] Amgen sued Chugai for infringement on its patent on a DNA sequence that encoded EPO, human erythropoeitin, a protein that stimulates the production of red blood cells. The court found that the patent covered the "novel *purified and isolated* sequence which codes for

EPO" (the italics are original). The purified DNA sequence, called cDNA, was the "invention," and the protein that it codes for, EPO, was covered under that patent.

Since *Amgen Inc. v Chugai Pharmaceutical Company*, the Patent Office has clarified this position and stated that "an isolated and purified DNA molecule that has the same sequence as a naturally occurring gene is eligible for a patent because… that DNA molecule does not occur in that isolated form in nature."[8]

Thus, biotechnology spokesmen are able to claim that patents on DNA don't actually cover DNA that is in the body: "There is a fair amount of confusion about what is actually being patented when one obtains a "gene" patent," Dennis Henner, Senior Vice President of Research at Genentech, Inc., says. "A 'gene' patent typically covers a specific chemical compound (i.e., a nucleic acid) that is produced using genetic information. Most frequently, the nucleic acid will have a physical structure that encodes the linear sequence of a particular protein. The physical structure of the nucleic will differ from what is found in the chromosome of an individual… A gene patent thus cannot give rights over a "gene" as it is found in your chromosomes."[9]

In other words, geneticists make a copy of the DNA in the laboratory and patent the chemicals in that copy.

Geneticists, however, are at odds as to just how "novel" the copied DNA is. Michael Finney, with the biotech company MJ Research, Inc. believes the Patent Office's claim that cDNA is a man-made invention is "incorrect, since in fact its structure is fixed and determined by mRNA, not by man… In fact, each cDNA is not a wholly new and "invented." compound, but rather the product of an obvious and predictable natural process… [cDNA] is a compound that may not exist in nature, but which is nonetheless an exact and predictable outcome of a standard laboratory procedure applied to compounds that do exist in nature… cDNAs encode the same protein as the native gene; therefore, any claims protecting a translated product of a cDNA are clearly claiming an obvious product of a naturally-occurring gene."[10]

Finney's final point is what is most important to us here: "…any claims protecting a translated product of a cDNA are clearly claiming an obvious product of a naturally-occurring gene." Theoretically, the copy is not the same as the naturally-occurring gene. But in the case of naturally-occurring DNA and cDNA the theoretical is irrelevant. Natural-occurring DNA does not exist outside the body (thus the term "naturally occurring"). If one wants to "take" a DNA sequence out of the body then one must make a copy. Therefore, a patent on a copied sequence, and its respective products, monopolizes all practical uses of the natural-occurring DNA—including research on the sequence. In practice, a patent claim over purified DNA is the same as a patent claim over what is found in the body.

The Patent Office's "purified and isolated" justification for life patents, therefore, is a rhetorical sleight of hand. It matters little that the exact chemicals being patented are not found in that exact form in the body, the patent clearly gives control over DNA that is in the body. Much like nations use maps to designate their sovereignty over natural landscapes, so biotech companies use patents on purified DNA to monopolize the naturally-occurring DNA in the body. The map is not the land itself, nevertheless, it clearly describes and gives the boundaries of the land. To claim what is on the map is to claim the land itself.

The phrases "life patents" or "patents on life" continue to be appropriate in describing patents that cover DNA, cDNA, or any other nucleotide sequences. These patents give proprietary control over a naturally occurring substance within our bodies. We have only to look at the examples given in the past two chapters to see that claiming the copy of the molecule means claiming the original in the body and all the right to research and exploit that original molecule.

As well, the claim that patents on purified molecular substances cannot give control over specific individual's body parts is a fallacy. Although none of us need to pay royalties on our BRCA genes or CCR5 that is in our bodies, the genetic make-up of the Greenberg family is now owned by one organization. The Greenbergs cannot offer their genetic material that is correlated with Canavan disease to any other research group without fear of patent infringement. The inhabitants of Tristan da Cunha cannot offer their molecular biology to another pharmaceutical company in order to study asthma.

An incredible amount of "novel" technology is used to map genomes and to produce genes and gene products in the laboratory. Ultimately, however, the "invention" produced—DNA—is not novel. Rather, it is something that nature invented long before humans learned its ingredients.

As Obvious as H_2O?

After novelty, the second element required by the Patent Office is non-obviousness. The idea is that things should not be patented that already have been in use for a long time, like your basic chair or wheel (though recently people have tried to patent the wheel). Also, one cannot patent something the use of which would be obvious to most anyone. You cannot patent a door stop made from a rock because it is obvious to most people that a rock could be used in that way.

Unlike a rock, nobody has actually seen a gene. Even with the most powerful microscopes, a gene cannot be visibly recognized. Still, scientists now have the technology to copy, purify, and map DNA. DNA, though a rather new discovery, is still a fact of nature, say some scientists, and is therefore obvious in its own right, even if we increasingly have gained the technology to identify more and more its components and functions. Michael Finney takes issue with the claimed non-obviousness of gene patents:

> ...The mere fact that a long-existing and long-rec-
> ognized compound can now be described based on its

nucleotide sequence does not create a patentable invention. To use a simple analogy, the compound called
"water" has been known to humans since the beginning of
time, but it was only in 1811 that Amedeo Avogadro first
determined that water can be described and expressed by
the chemical formula H_2O. Identifying that water is comprised of two hydrogen atoms and one oxygen atom was a
great advancement in scientific knowledge; it would be
absurd, however, to take the position that Avogadro, upon
making this discovery, was thereupon entitled to a patent
on water. This is, however, what the PTO appears to be
allowing when it purports to grant a patent on a known
compound merely because that compound has now been
analyzed and its nucleotide sequence identified.

"Sequencing of genes, while [it] is useful from a scientific
and research standpoint, does not create anything new," Finney
continues. "Indeed, once the sequencing process became highly
automated, identifying the sequence of any gene, cDNA, purified DNA, EST or other DNA-derived sequence became
extremely obvious to the point of banality."[11]

In essence, DNA sequences are as obvious as rocks and
water. Not only have they always been there and nothing new
is created when one discovers their chemical compositions, but
even the chemical compositions of DNA sequences are obvious
to most working geneticists.

Modern biotech laboratories don't look like your seventh
grade science class. Rooms are filled with million dollar robotic
sequencing machines that work at decoding genes. Particularly
in the case of DNA patents on SNPs (single nucleotide poly-
morphisms) and ESTs (expressed sequence tags), the race to
claim a patent on DNA depends less on the intellectual brain-
power of your researchers and more on the megabytes of your
computer. The patent goes to the researcher not with the most
inventive mind, but to the researcher with the fastest computer
and the most efficient intellectual property lawyers. It's the gold

digger with the back-hoe who wins over the prospector wielding a pick axe. We might marvel at the inventor of the back-hoe, but surely that should not give the back-hoe user the patent rights to gold.

Scientists who are suspicious of the inventiveness that DNA patents award include some distinguished heavyweights in the field. Harold Varmus, former director of the National Institutes of Health (NIH), told Congress that in his opinion "many of the thousands of gene patents that have been awarded appear to reward unduly the preliminary and frankly obvious work of determining DNA sequence and to diminish the value of the innovative scientific work required ultimately to determine gene function and medical utility."[12]

The College of American Pathologists put it succinctly in its position paper against gene patents: "Information derived from mapping the human genome represents a naturally occurring, fundamental level of knowledge, which is not invented by man and should not be patented."[13]

There is still another criterion on which a potential patent is judged: utility. How do DNA sequences fare on this score?

How Do You Want to Use My Genes?

After novelty and non-obviousness, the third and last element required to award a patent is the utility requirement. Utility—what an invention actually does—is what differentiates "art" from an invention. You may be able to convince someone that a novel, non-obvious combination of wood and chicken wire is art, but if you cannot prove that it actually does something then you do not have an invention.

Even within the biotechnology industry, there are doubts whether certain patents that cover biological material meet the utility requirement. Gene patents fall into three general fields, each of which can be considered in turn: First, patents on DNA sequences in which no clear or specific utility is known; second, patents on sequences in which some functions are known; and, lastly, patents in which an actual therapeutic use is specified; i.e., in which the biological material itself can be used as a "drug." For clarity, we'll label these fields broad-utility patents, disease gene patents, and therapeutic patents respectively.

A prime example of a broad-utility patent in which little was known about its function, at least at the time of the application, is Human Genome Sciences's CCR5 patent discussed in Chapter One. It is also a prime example of what Harold Varmus was talking about in his quote above. One company, HGS, did the preliminary "and frankly obvious" work of determining a DNA sequence. By awarding the patent to HGS, the Patent Office diminished "the value of the innovative scientific work required ultimately to determine gene function and utility." In this case, innovative work was done by NIH scientists and their affiliates to discover that CCR5 had some correlation to AIDS. HGS, on the other hand, was granted the patent control over all research into the relationship between AIDS and CCR5 simply by stating the rather obvious fact that CCR5 could be a receptor for a virus.

Hundreds of gene patents have been awarded on DNA molecules that have been sequenced but whose function is not known or is known only in a very general sense. Thousands more are pending.

Jorge Goldstein, a patent attorney for Human Genome Sciences, justifies these patents: "In chemical patent law for 100 years, everywhere in the world, if you discover a compound that has any use, even a marginal use, you are entitled to a patent on the compound... If you use it, you are going to have to pay me a royalty, even though I did not discover its hot commercial use, but a marginal one. That's been the law for a hundred years. Biotech hasn't changed anything."[14]

"We did real biology. We didn't just find a gene and patent it," HGS CEO William A. Haseltine says about the CCR5 patent. "In this case, we were clever enough to guess right that this is a viral receptor."[15]

These patents have made many researchers in the biotech and pharmaceutical industries very nervous, as well as their academic and government counterparts. Most of these patents are known as composition patents, that is, they cover a chemical composition and give the rights to that composition. If other researchers are working with the composition, but find a different use for it, they can apply for what is known as a process patent. But the process patent holder still has to pay a licensing fee to the composition patent holder in order to work with the composition. Often in the case of these broad patents on genes, however, the utility requirement is so general and abstract that the original patent covers most processes. Thus, the patent for CCR5 mentioned that the cell receptor may be a receptor for viruses and therefore any research with any virus and its interaction with CCR5 will be covered by the patent.

It's easy to see why people working in the industry are nervous. If you are studying AIDS or tuberculosis and you are trying to figure out how these diseases interact with the body's cells, you may discover that a certain gene plays a role in the interaction. But then you must find out who owns the gene, how broad their patent is, and who to pay royalties to before proceeding. To make matters worse, what the patent covers or not is often open to interpretation. As we will see, working out this interpretation more often than not occurs in the context of million-dollar lawsuits.

Biotechnology representatives complained loudly about the broad utility guidelines to the Patent Office in a meeting in 1994. For the next few years, the Patent Office analyzed and guided public discussions on its utility requirements for gene patents. In January 2001, the Patent Office published new guidelines for determining the usefulness or "utility" of an invention. Although the new guidelines applied to all invention applications, they clearly targeted DNA patents in response to industry complaints. Although it appears that the guidelines make it harder to receive patents on genes—for example on expressed tag sequences (ESTs), sequenced gene fragments with no known utility—it is still too early to see just how restrictive the new guidelines will be. The guidelines demand that an invention have a "credible" and "real world" utility.

Intellectual property lawyer Warren Kaplan and Tufts professor of environmental policy Sheldon Krimsky, however, say the new guidelines may not have the desired affect of restricting patents on genes with no known utility. "We may be surprised to see how many DNA, protein, EST or SNP inventions have 'credible' utility," they wrote in an article examining the guidelines.[16]

Ultimately, it may be too late to put restrictions on these broad-utility gene patents. "It may be that most of these human genes have already been published, filed as patent applications, or issued as patents," Krimsky and Kaplan note. Instead, the guidelines will become more important as biotechnology company turn to patents on the proteins that are encoded by genes.

What's The Use of Disease Genes?

Other patents on DNA do a better job of meeting the utility requirement by presenting a "real world" utility. This type of patent falls into the second field of gene patents. Patents on disease genes are a good example of this. The patent is awarded because the company or university has proven that a particular DNA sequence has a correlation to a disease or condition. Even if this correlation is somewhat miniscule—for example, BRCA1 and BRCA2 correlate to only 5% of breast cancer cases—a patent can be awarded because the researchers have shown that they can develop a genetic test or use the gene to research therapies.

It is easier to see why disease gene patents fulfill the utility requirement (even if they continue to fail the "novelty" requirement). The company or university has theoretically "discovered" a chemical composition in the body which has some association with a disease or condition. A real world use is seen explicitly. However, the same problems arise as with the patents on DNA that patentees know little about. Even if a company or university claims to know certain characteristics of a gene, by giving a monopoly of that gene to one research group the patent hinders other researchers from finding other functions, uses, or correlations to other diseases or conditions with that gene.

A fascinating example of this is the idea that a mutated gene which may make an individual more susceptible to one disease may simultaneously prove to make the individual less susceptible to other harmful health conditions. Harvard epidemiologist Walter C. Willett discovered this proved true in a number of studies: "Specific genotype can be beneficial for one outcome (cancer) but detrimental for another (birth defects)."[17] What some researchers may view as a harmful genetic mutation may turn out to be lifesaving genetic condition.

Entities that claim patents on a gene with a particular utility is akin to a company that tries to patent the word "the." The company claims to have isolated the word by taking it out of the sentence that usually surrounds it. The company has discovered that it can give a description of the word "the"—it has three letters in a specific order, etc. In this way, the company has also proven it is a new and novel invention because "the" does not occur naturally in language without at least a noun. The company says its researchers have isolated and copied the word. As well, with its computers, the company claims to have discovered that the word "the" occurs in, say, 5% of sentences that are "soothing." The company says it has found a correlation between "the" and soothing sentences. In its patent application, therefore, the company claims that the "utility" of the word "the" is that it has a correlation to soothing sentences. This company hopes to produce products from the word "the," perhaps a whole series of sentences that are soothing. As an analogy to life patents, this hypothetical "utility" of the word "the" would be enough evidence for the Patent Office to issue a patent on it.

But the word "the" is such a basic word that monopolizing its use, even if it's a helpful use, would dam up using it in other contexts. Further, like things from nature, why would we want to patent words at all?

The point is, again, knowledge about our DNA is still upstream knowledge. By allowing one company that knows one way to use it to claim that DNA, patents put a market on upstream knowledge that should be shared and explored by as many researchers as possible.

The Protein That Knew Too Much and Other Therapeutic Patents

Finally, a third field of gene patents contains therapeutic patents. Therapeutic patents cover molecular material found in the body in which the molecule itself has a very specific therapeutic use. The best example of this is Amgen's Epogen drug, made from a purified protein found in the kidneys called erythropoietin or EPO. Amgen's EPO patents stand as the one biotechnology success story that has actually made real money for a company by the sale of a real therapeutic product to actual patients. The EPO protein stimulates production of red blood cells, and Amgen seized it as a therapy to combat anemia, the decrease in red blood cells seen most commonly in patients with kidney disease.[18] With 100,000 kidney dialysis patients in this country and nearly 5 million people who suffer from anemia, this drug can help many.

To have as large a monopoly as possible, companies and universities often strengthen their intellectual property by applying for "cluster patents," patents that surround every aspect of a specific piece of biology. Successfully using five cluster patents on the EPO protein, Amgen's patents monopolize nearly every aspect of the EPO protein. Another example of the use of cluster patents is Myriad which has at least eight patents covering genetic material with correlations to breast cancer.[19]

Amgen's EPO patents, and other similar therapeutic patents, fulfill the utility requirement of the Patent Office as the biological molecules they cover clearly serve a function, i.e., the protein itself is a drug. Historically, the EPO patents are similar to patents given on penicillin or insulin—although they are taken from nature, they are purified and used as a specific treatment.

The difference, however, between the EPO patents and historical patents on chemicals found in nature, is how broad the Amgen patents are and just how much of the "native" molecular materials it monopolizes. A brief look at the history of Amgen's EPO demonstrates how, using this monopoly, the patent has been used to halt innovative research that would make the erythropoietin therapy more effective, less expensive, and safer for thousands of people.

Amgen did not even discover erythropoietin first (which calls into question, once again, life patent proponents who say life patents give credit where credit is due). Eugene Goldwasser originally isolated EPO in a University of Chicago laboratory in 1976. Goldwasser asked the university to apply for a patent on it, but the idea of patenting molecular biology had not yet come into vogue and the university did not answer his calls.[20] Nor was Amgen the first to try using EPO to treat amenia.[21] Nevertheless, as we have seen, often it is not the prime researchers who are honored with a patent, but those with the best lawyers.

In 1983, Amgen scientists successfully reproduced EPO in the laboratory.[22] The small upstart biotech company began working towards a patent, already in a race with others who were on the EPO kick.

In 1989, before the patent was even awarded, Amgen was in court fighting for its "property." While Amgen had patented the process for reproducing EPO in the laboratory, another company, Genentech, had been granted a patent on the EPO molecule itself. Amgen sued Genentech, who counter-sued, but said they would settle for cross licensing in which both companies could have rights to the protein. Amgen refused.

"Amgen executives insist a principle is at stake," *The Wall Street Journal* reported. "Their company was first to clone the EPO gene [referring not to a gene but to a protein], so it should reap the rewards. 'This is what U.S. patent laws are all about; otherwise, forget rewarding innovation for small entrepreneurs,' Mr. Rathmann [Chairman of Amgen] argues."[23]

At the same time, Amgen was in court against their marketing partner, Johnson and Johnson's Ortho. This time, Amgen was refusing to settle a licensing agreement for EPO. A judge halted the FDA process for EPO, delaying its release to the public by two months. Amgen's stock rose and fell like a roller coaster.

Amgen finally got EPO off the ground and out the door and it became the dream protein everyone had imagined. Dialysis patients found renewed energy—for $8,000 a year. Amgen found renewed financial energy—$4 billion a year in sales.

Amgen applied for and was granted numerous cluster patents on the protein itself, the process for copying the protein, the gene that encodes the protein, and host cells where the gene is found. These patents cover nearly every element of the biological material, from its chemical composition to laboratory processes for studying it.

In 1998, Amgen's market share was threatened again. This time, Lawrence Berkeley Laboratory (LBL) discovered a "protein binding factor" that would keep the EPO from being excreted into the urine of patients. The LBL discovery could keep natural EPO in the body longer, lowering the patient's required dosage of Amgen's EPO. It was easy to see how using this factor could cut into the sales of Amgen's prize product.

However, the protein binding factor could only work with EPO—and, as we have seen, Amgen owned all the rights to the protein. Other biotech companies that wanted to test LBL's discovery were afraid of lawsuits from Amgen. Amgen itself refused to test or market the LBL's discovery, even though it would have made EPO treatments cheaper for thousands who could not keep EPO in the body naturally.

"Amgen wasn't interested [in the discovery] because it would decrease their lucrative market for EPO," an employee of LBL stated at the time.[24]

Consumer activist Ralph Nader wrote President Clinton about Amgen's refusal, demanding that the government reevaluate the Patent Office's policy on life patents. "They're [Amgen] in a conflict where their desire to maximize their profits is damaging the interests of their patients," Nader said in an interview.[25]

During the summer of 2000, Amgen found itself in court again defending its EPO patent. This time, a small company, Transkaryotic Therapies Inc., had found another way of reproducing EPO. In fact, while Amgen produced the protein in hamster cells, Transkaryotic had found a way of "turning on" the gene that made EPO in human cells, a technology that was not available at the time of Amgen's original EPO patent. Transkaryotic felt that its process was significantly different from Amgen's. Even the resulting EPO was slightly different from the EPO Amgen had described in its patents.

According to the lawyers for Transkaryotic, Amgen's broad EPO patent claims were akin to Columbus declaring ownership of the entire world simply because he discovered a few small islands. "No doubt his discovery was profound, even revolutionary," the lawyers said. "But he indisputably did not discover Asia, Africa, Australia or Antarctica."[26]

"This case poses a fundamental question of the biotechnology age," Transkaryotic's lawyers stated in a brief. "Just how far can a patent extend beyond what it discloses to the public as its invention, to preempt future progress and innovation by others?"[27]

Transkaryotic lost. Their stocks fell 50%. Amgen's stocks shot up from $7.44 to $67.44 that same day.[28] The real losers, however, were the patients who may have benefited from Transkaryotic's technological advances.

In both the Transkaryotic case and the Lawrence Berkeley Laboratory innovation, a life patent was used in exactly the opposite manner for which patents were intended: It stifled innovation. The problem was that Amgen held a number of patents not simply on a chemical composition—isolated and purified EPO—but also controlled the protein in the body (and the DNA that encoded it and the cell that held the DNA, etc.) and therefore in effect had a monopoly on all aspects of EPO and anything that affected EPO.

Amgen's life-saving protein is the culmination of many years of government perks, not to mention the political favors the company gained by its intensive lobbying in Washington. In 1989, Amgen was granted "Orphan Drug status" for their EPO by the FDA. Congress had passed the Orphan Drug Act a few years before in order to give broad intellectual property rights and tax breaks for the development of drugs that would help people who had rare diseases. Through the orphan drug status, Amgen gained market exclusivity that helped them defeat competing EPO patents in lawsuits.[29] Amgen also received tax relief for manufacturing goods in Puerto Rico and from the Research and Development Tax Credit.

The EPO patent brings up an important paradox: Even if one accepts that certain life patents meet the Patent Office's utility requirement, these life patents ultimately fail the intention underlying the creation of a patent system declared in Article I, Section 8 of the U.S. Constitution: stimulating the progress of science, promoting the public good, and protecting inventors' rights. Amgen's EPO patents appear to contradict all three of these Constitutional mandates. We will examine these mandates more closely in Chapter Six.

Life patents usually fail to meet the three criteria of novelty, non-obviousness and utility. Even when some life patents appear to meet these criteria, they can be so broad as to defeat rather than protect innovation. But what about objects that don't occur naturally, like genetically modified crops or animals? How do we assess those patent claims?

GMOs: Dr. Frankenstein's Patented Pets

As we have seen, the first life patent ever granted was on a genetically modified organism. The Supreme Court decided that Chakrabarty's genetically altered bacteria was patentable in 1980. In 1987, the first patent on an animal was granted on a genetically modified oyster. This was followed by the first patent on a mammal in 1988 for the Harvard Mouse, "invented" by Harvard researchers, Phil Leder and Timothy Stewart. Leder and Stewart inserted a gene that made the mice, and its progeny, more susceptible to breast cancer. The "utility" of this mouse, then, was for scientific research into breast cancer.

As with all life patents, it is difficult to get an accurate picture of how many genetically modified animals have been patented since, but within one year of the Harvard Mouse there were patents granted on "106 mice, 9 rats, 9 rabbits, 8 sheep, 8 pigs, 7 cows, 7 goats, and one each of a nematode, bird, fish, guinea pig, abalone, canine, and turkey hen."[30]

In applying the Patent Office's three requirements for an invention to GMOs, we seem to easily fulfill at least two of them in most cases. GMOs are not obvious. If you ran into a mouse in your kitchen, you probably would not think to manipulate its genes to make it more susceptible to cancer. Further, researchers can prove the utility of modified organisms simply by claiming they are research tools to study how certain genes act when modified or combined with a different species' genes, etc. We will look at life patents as research tools a little later on.

It is the Patent Office's first requirement, the newness or

novelty of these organisms, where there is a question. The Patent Office has applied the idea that the "hand of man" has been used to such an extent in these organisms that they can indeed be considered inventions. This reasoning is a matter of debate.

Key Dismukes, Study Director for the Committee on Vision of the National Academy of Sciences, replies to Patent Office's "hand of man" justification for Chakrabarty's invention:

> Let us get one thing straight: Ananda Chakrabarty did not create a new form of life; he merely intervened in the normal processes by which strains of bacteria exchange genetic information, to produce a new strain with an altered metabolic pattern. "His" bacterium lives and reproduces itself under the forces that guide all cellular life. Recent advances in recombinant DNA techniques allow more direct biochemical manipulation of bacterial genes than Chakrabarty employed, but these too are only modulations of biological processes. We are incalculably far away from being able to create life de novo [from scratch], and for that I am profoundly grateful. The argument that the bacterium is Chakrabarty's handiwork and not nature's wildly exaggerates human power and displays the same hubris and ignorance of biology that have had such devastating impact on the ecology of our planet.[31]

Put another way by Leon R. Kass, Chairman of the President's Council on Bioethics:[32] "Chakrabarty did not himself create the new bacterium. Rather, he played matchmaker for a shotgun wedding and the selector of its progeny, while the living organisms did the work."

Others, such as Vandana Shiva, Director of the Research Foundation for Science, Technology and Natural Resource Policy in New Delhi, have questioned the inconsistent rhetoric used to support the novel requirement: "When property rights to life forms are claimed, it is on the basis of them being new, novel, not occurring in nature. However, when environmental-ists state that being 'not natural,' genetically modified organisms will have special ecological impacts, which need to be known and assessed, and for which the 'owners' need to take responsibility, the argument is that they are not new or unnatural. These organisms are 'natural,' and hence safe. The issue of biosafety is therefore treated as unnecessary. Thus when biological organisms are to be owned, they are treated as not natural; when the responsibility for consequences of releasing genetically modified organisms is to be owned, they are treated as natural."[33]

As we found with patented genes and genomes, patents on GMOs are also surprisingly broad: "The mouse patent is not for one specific mouse," Harvard biologist Ruth Hubbard and Tufts University professor Sheldon Krimsky explain, "but for a strain of mice, no two individuals of which are identical, and which can go on producing changes from generation to generation. The patent covers the genetically modified mouse, all of its progeny and all of their progeny for seventeen years, much longer than the life span of the "manufactured" mouse. Can Drs. Leder and Stewart really be said to have manufactured generations of mice because they operated on the eggs of one?"[34]

The Harvard Mouse patent caused much more of a public uproar than the previous patents on genetically modified bacteria and purified and isolated DNA. The Animal Legal Defense Fund joined with others in a lawsuit against the Patent Office and its policy of granting patents on mammals, but the suit was dismissed. Among other things, animal rights advocates take issue with the fact that some genetically modified animals have been modified specifically to suffer, as is the case of the Harvard Mouse that is destined to die of cancer. Whether we should create animals that suffer is a separate issue from what concerns us here, but it should be noted that the animal rights position is one of many opinions that is not heard when the Patent Office hands out patents.

As mentioned before, the Harvard Mouse, and many sub-sequent GMOs, met the utility requirement by the claim that they were "research tools" that could be used to conduct further research on diseases, conditions, or genes themselves. Other life patents have used the same utility argument, for example expressed sequence tags (ESTs), "uncharacteristic" sequenced DNA fragments of which little is known. The argument is that research using these tools will advance innovation. But a closer look reveals a more complex picture.

Stuart Little as Research Tool

Any tool is a weapon if you hold it right.
—Ani DiFranco[35]

In 1998, the NIH created a working group to examine problems arising from studies with patented materials, including patented DNA. The NIH group surveyed 32 academic institu-tions and 26 private firms, many of which were conducting research with taxpayers' money.[36] The working group analyzed "the problems encountered in the dissemination and use of pro-prietary research tools." The NIH working group found:

- Research that required negotiating, reviewing, and admin-istrating the access to research tools took too much time and money, slowing down the actual scientific research.

- Licensing terms for patented materials were not standard-ized, making each licensing agreement newly complicated.

- Institutions that sought profit from their patented materi-als were generally unwilling to make them freely available. These patent owning researchers limited who had access to the research materials, restricted how they were used, and restricted or delayed disclosure of the results of their own research.

- Some researchers could not afford the fees demanded for

using these patented materials.

The working group concluded "we have detected considerable dissatisfaction with the current operation of the patent system in biomedical research from many quarters, suggesting that there may be considerable room for improvement."

From its study, the working group recommended that research should be conducted with "free dissemination of research materials" whenever possible. The NIH's authority, however, only covers organizations that work directly under its control. It has little or no position of authority on organizations funded partly or in full by private companies.

Again, we are not talking about mousetraps but about research tools that will assist in discovering the causes and perhaps the cures of diseases. It is as if we found that mice were carrying a deadly disease, but the companies that had patents on mousetraps did not allow anyone to use the traps in the fight against the disease. Or, faced with this imaginary mouse-carrying disease, the patent holders on mousetraps would not allow anyone to make improvements on the invention. This is analogous to what is happening with a creature called the "Cre-*loxP* Mouse."

The DuPont company owns the exclusive license to the Harvard Mouse. They also own the rights to another, less educated-sounding patented mouse called the Cre-*loxP* Mouse. Although the mouse attracted little attention when it was first introduced in 1985, it has now become an important element in many genetic studies. With the Cre-*loxP* Mouse, researchers can delete a target gene in the mouse's offspring—a sort of "natural" gene splicing—and create other genetically modified mice. The Cre-*loxP* Mouse is therefore a starting point for many studies and the technique itself has been improved upon in taxpayer-funded labs.

It's one thing to patent a mouse and charge royalties on offspring, but DuPont's patent extends far beyond this basic idea of charging on a per-mouse basis. In 1997, DuPont decided to enforce its patent and set up a licensing system. Under the system, researchers pay royalties on any commercial discoveries they make with the mouse. At the time, Harold Varmus, director of the National Institutes of Health, took issue with the licensing structure, believing that it would "seriously impede further basic research and thwart the development of future technologies that will benefit the public."

The patent claims on research tools were becoming problematic, even within his own organization, Varmus claimed. "There are investigators here who would like to seek intellectual protections for everything they do, and I don't find it very appealing."[37]

Other researchers found the same problems in surprising contexts, such as academia where, at one time, tools which advanced research were proudly shared. "I think patenting this kind of technology [research tools] is unwarranted and damaging to science," Nobel prize winner and Stanford professor of Biochemistry Paul Berg says. "This practice is emerging as a terrible precedent. Academic institutions are becoming so hungry for revenue that they are trying to patent everything."[38]

Referring to genetically modified mice as "research tools" neutralizes the image of such creatures into inanimate objects. The fact is that these living things breed and impact the environment around them. One person's research tool can become another person's nightmare. A looming question concerning GMOs is how safe they are.

Real World Utility: It Kills

Imagine you paid good money for a new ACME brand refrigerator and then, one day about a year later, it suddenly broke down. Chances are you would not go back and buy the same brand of refrigerator. But what if there was a monopoly and only ACME brand refrigerators were sold? So you go back and get another refrigerator and a year later, sure enough, it breaks down again. You do this for a few more years and then you find out that ACME deliberately built in obsolescence. Within a year you will always have to buy another one.

This is a good business strategy for ACME because, by creating demand year after year, it guarantees that ACME will always sell its refrigerators, no matter how poorly they are made. Such monopolies rightfully anger consumers and provide one reason why there are anti-trust laws.

A refrigerator is one thing, but imagine you were sold a similar self-destructing product except that you could not make a living without this product. Like a car or a computer. Now imagine you were sold a self-destructing product that you couldn't live without. Like a pacemaker.

Those ACME refrigerators are similar to a new genetic innovation called "Terminator seeds." Terminator seeds are genetically altered seeds that are sterile and do not produce new seeds. Terminator seeds are seeds that would force farmers to buy new seeds from a company every year, instead of re-using seeds from their harvest as has been done by humankind for millennia. It may seem that this is not a life and death matter like a pacemaker that wears out. Yet the threat of Terminator seeds far overshadows any threat by short-lived pacemakers. 1.4 billion people depend on farm-saved seeds.[39] In India, 70% of seed supply comes from farmers' harvested seeds.[40] In other words, billions of people eat and live because of the ancient practice of seed saving.

The Rural Advancement Foundation International (RAFI) reported in a 2002 newsletter: "When Terminator technology came to public light in March 1998, 'suicide seeds' shattered the myth that commercial biotechnology aims to feed hungry people."[41]

Indeed, in the late 90s there was a large outcry against the technology. RAFI, farm organizations, and representatives of the global south decried the Terminator technology when it first was made public. Within a year, Monsanto, an agrochemcial company, promised not to commercialize the seed because of overwhelming public pressure.

But Monsanto has since been bought out by another agrochemical company, Pharmacia, which has *not* taken a similar vow. "Contrary to what some of these companies have pledged in the past, the Gene Giants are refining the technology and moving forward to commercialize Terminator seeds," says Hope Shand, Research Director of the Action Group on Erosion, Technology, and Conservation (ETC).[42]

One might think that the ACME refrigerator analogy doesn't quite correspond with the Terminator technology. After all, in this open world economy, once farmers know that a seed self destructs, they will simply buy from another company. But as we saw in Chapter Two, the world's seeds are now almost completely controlled by five companies: Pharmacia (Monsanto), Syngenta, DuPont, Dow Chemical, and Aventis.

By 2001, four of these five had taken out patents on terminator seeds—most of which were granted *after* Monsanto promised not to commercialize.[43]

Julie Delahanty of ETC believes that this is a clear sign that these companies are bent on commercializing terminator seeds, regardless of it ecological implications:[44]

"Obviously, we can't rely on the goodwill of multinational seed and agrochemical corporations to safeguard the public from the threat of Terminator seeds. If these companies are serious about abandoning the Terminator technology, they should surrender their patents to the control of the UN Food & Agriculture Organization, agreeing not to develop the technology themselves, nor allow others access to their technologies."

RAFI observed in a 2001: "The ultimate goal of genetic seed sterility is neither biosafety nor agronomic benefits, but bioserfdom."[45]

As one might have gathered, many of the agrochemical companies dallying in genetically modified crops are the chemical companies of old and companies such as Monsanto do not have a good track record in regards to respecting public safety. In 2002, Monsanto and Pharmacia were successfully sued by a group of citizens in Anniston, Alabama for polluting the town with polychlorinated biphyls (PCBs) over a number of decades. The Anniston contamination of PCBs is considered the worst PCB site in the world and as many as 20,000 residents will have their cases heard over the coming years.[46] The most frightening aspect of the Anniston case is the fact that for years Monsanto deliberately covered up the extent of the pollution and the health danger. Among other charges, the jury found the company guilty of "outrage," i.e. conduct "so outrageous in character and extreme in degree as to go beyond all possible bounds of decency so as to be regarded as atrocious and utterly intolerable in civilized society."

For the Environmental Working Group, the Anniston story stands as "a cautionary tale. If Monsanto hid what it knew about its toxic pollution for decades, what is the company hiding from the public now? This question seems particularly important as this powerful company asks the world to trust it with a worldwide, high-stakes gamble with the environmental consequences of its genetically modified organisms."[47]

Farmers threatened by Terminator seeds, Native Americans who harvest wild rice, and concerned consumers of GMO foods all share two basic fears about genetically engineered plants and animals. The first is that GMOs will get out into the natural environment, pollinate or breed with natural-occurring species, and thus destroy nature as we know it. We will not be able to look around, never mind eat, anything but that which has been touched by the "hand of man." Everything we see will be owned through patents, since everything—our farm animals, our crops, perhaps our forests and flowers—will all be considered "novel" in its genetically engineered state. Fifteen years ago, author and environmentalist Bill McKibben warned in *The End of Nature* of the first end of nature, described as global climate changes threatening our ecosystem. The "second end of nature," McKibben warned, would be the takeover by bioengineered life: "We will live, eventually, in a shopping mall, where every feature is designed for our delectation."[48]

The second fear concerning GMOs is related to the first. Many believe there may be unexpected dangers with GMOs that scientists have yet to discover. (Or, in the case of Terminator seeds, fully predictable dangers that we already know.) Our tinkering with "research tools" for scientific advancement may set off a chain reaction that could culminate in an ecological disaster.

Is this just the old argument that we must not play God? Or is the fear more justified?

Two controversial studies released in 1999 fuel this fear of GMOs. One found that soybean seeds that had been modified with a Brazilian nut gene caused allergic reactions in people with Brazil nut allergies. Another discovered that genetically altered corn killed monarch butterfly larvae and threatened to decimate the entire species.[49] Scientists are at odds on the results of these studies and we are likely to see many more studies in the coming years with contradictory and controversial evidence.

The worries about genetically modified plants and animals are not placated by the meager controls put on such organisms. Yes, the FDA now requires that genetically modified food should be labeled if it is thought to be a safety risk—but it is up to the company that makes GM foods to discover such risks.[50] For some, this is like having the tobacco companies monitor the risks of smoking.

There is much more extensive scientific and philosophical literature elsewhere on the effects of GMOs. Our question here is should GMOs—like Terminator seeds—be allowed to be patented? Within the requirement of utility, shouldn't moral and ecological implications of the granting of a patent be considered? Historically, it was implicit in the patent process that the inventions be beneficial to society, not harmful. Justice Story made this point in 1817 in *Lowell v. Lewis*, ruling that an "invention should not be frivolous or injurious to the well-being, good policy, or sound morals of society. The word 'useful,' therefore, is incorporated into the act in contradistinction to mischievous or immoral."[51]

The Patent Office, on the other hand, says it is not its job to judge on the ethics of a biotech "inventions." Thus the inventions continue apace, regardless of the risk.

Patentability

We have seen a wide range of things associated with life or actual life forms that have been patented—mice, corn, rice, tuberculosis, ESTs and STPs, genes and genomes. Some see these things as research tools, other see them as upstream knowledge, still others see them as life or the stuff of life. According to the Patent Office, all of these meet its requirements to be called an invention.

We have also seen a list of problems that have come with these patents. Each of these problems, however, the Patent Office either cannot or simply refuses to deal with.

Because of restrictive licensing, some life patents clearly go against the Constitutional mandate that patents should stimulate innovation, but the Patent Office says it has nothing to do with that: "Whether something is patentable subject matter is a related but entirely different issue from whether it will be licensed to ensure appropriate access by researchers," former Patent Office director Dickinson says. "As I have described, the USPTO's chief duty is to determine whether an invention claimed in a given patent application meets the legal criteria for patentability."[52]

Some life patents, such as those on Amgen's EPO, are so broad that their granting means years of litigious dispute and more delays in research. As Robert Abbott, former CEO of the biotech company Viagene, says, "People will challenge patents that are too broad and it will be worked out, but at a cost of millions of dollars and thousands of man hours."[53]

But the Patent Office says that is none of its business: "After patents have issued, there's very little our office can do," Dickinson says. "If there is a problem here, and it's not clear yet whether there is or is not, but if there is a problem here, the court's job is to look at all of this and say that some patents may have issued inappropriately."[54]

Some life patents cover plants or organisms that could unleash an ecological danger if they were to escape into nature, but the Patent Office need not worry about that. Their job is simply to decide if a claimed invention is novel, non-obvious, and has utility. It is not up to them to decide if an invention is dangerous or life-threatening.

Others believe that all life patents, even those that cover GMOs, give the "hand of man" too much credit for "inventing" natural-occurring molecular structures, plants, and animals. "The humans, animals, microorganisms, and plants comprising life on earth are part of the natural world into which we were all born," a coalition of fourteen environmental, indigenous people, and human rights groups wrote in 1995. "The conversion of these life forms, their molecules or parts in to corporate property through patent monopolies is counter to the interests of the peoples of this country and of the world."[55]

"We believe that humans and animals are creations of God, not humans, and as such should not be patented as human inventions," leaders of 80 different religious faiths announced in 1995.[56]

But the Patent Office does not have to listen to these voices. The rhetoric of the Patent Office reflects the rhetoric of the biotech companies. Genes and GMOs aren't life, they say. "Genes are basically chemicals," Dickinson says. "Complex chemicals to be sure, but chemicals nevertheless."

As we have seen, there are many different kinds of life

patents. Some, like patents on quinoa or wild rice, appear to have little to do with inventiveness and much more to do with theft and willful monopolies over living things. Other life patents, however, are less clear. Some people who may be against patenting mice might think that Amgen should get some kind of protection for its Epogen drug. What is clear across the wide range of these examples, however, is that the Patent Office is not the right vehicle for making these decisions.

How, one may ask, did the Patent Office alone get the power to decide that genes are merely chemicals, easily patentable, and that animals are merely research tools, patentable as well?

At first, through *Chakrabarty*, the Patent Office was led by the Supreme Court, but only in a legal sense. The court said a GMO was patentable under the requirements of the Patent Office, but the justices left it to Congress to decide whether GMOs—and all life forms—*should* be patentable. Judge Berger, who presided over *Chakrabarty*, hinted at the need for a closer look by Congress of the negative implications of certain patents in his ruling. As he saw it, the court's job was merely to decide if Chakrabarty met the utility requirement to be a patent, not if, ultimately, genetically altered life forms should be patentable. Congress could, Berger wrote, "amend §101 [on utility] so as to exclude from patent protection organisms produced by genetic engineering." Berger understood that Congress could do so under the same statute that does not allow nuclear weapons to be patented.[57]

In other words, the Supreme Court decision was not a decision in regards to whether patents on life forms and genes should be allowed. It is as if you tried to patent a nuclear weapon. Although it has never been attempted, it is quite possible, under the Supreme Court's reasoning, that a nuclear weapon is patentable because it meets the Patent Office's three requirements of novel, non-obvious, and having real world utility. But the real question is not whether a nuclear weapon meets the requirements of the Patent Office, it is whether a nuclear weapon *should* be allowed to be patented. And, of course, Congress has made an actual law that states that nuclear weapons should not and cannot be patented, regardless of their "patentability." Congress has yet to consider the question of whether patents on life forms and genes should be allowed, despite the Supreme Court's suggestion.

As well, the Supreme Court had no idea of the consequential floodgates that would open because of that decision. The court did not know that by saying a microorganism was patentable, the Patent Office would soon be granting patents on swaths of DNA found in our body, plants found throughout the world, and whole generations of mammals. The Patent Office has since made decisions on its own, citing old court cases, most of which have nothing to do with genes and GMOs. A few Congressional leaders have asked that the policy of granting life patents be looked at more carefully, but little came of these requests. And the Patent Office does not allow input from any outside parties—including the public—when it considers whether to grant a patent. The Patent Office has basically had no guidance from Congress and the tax-paying public in over 20 years of life patents.

Freed from consideration of the consequences, isolated from Congress and public debate, the Patent Office makes decisions alone on so-called inventions that are stifling science and "changing the nature of nature."[58]

What drove the Patent Office to make these decisions? The answer is pretty clear: the biotech industry. Life patents, the industry has said, is our life blood. Take them away and the whole biotech project collapses. But why—if life patents stifle innovation and slow scientific advancement—does the biotech industry support them so strongly? The answer here is money. Scientists, and the companies and universities that employ them, they say, will not have the incentive to study without the promise of financial reward that life patents promise.

This is a rather pessimistic view of the human spirit and the quest for knowledge. It is more than likely, as it always has been, that scientists, universities, and even companies would continue to do research even without the need to own the basic materials they are looking at (and any questionable financial returns that may come from them). It is true, however, that investors would not have been so keen on sinking millions into the biotechnology industry in the past twenty years if that industry did not have life patents to advertise. Life patents were seen by stockholders as signs that biotech companies would soon start making money. Numerous press releases that bragged about a company's life patents raised much of the financing necessary for the creation of hundreds of small research companies. The idea was that these patents covered real inventions that could be bought and sold and that this was where the profit was going to come from.

It is an irony of history, then, that the abolition of life patents—or, at the very least, strong governmental restrictions on them—is now necessary for the biotech industry's survival.

As we will see in the next chapter, greed got us into the business of granting patents on life. Greed may now get us out.

CHAPTER FIVE

Lifeblood of a Dying Industry

Time for a New Cure?

> Patents are the lifeblood of the industry and are crucial to spurring innovation and incenting [sic] companies to make the necessary significant investments to bring drugs to market.
>
> —Art Levinson, CEO of
> Genentech, Inc.[1]

> In legislative debate, the economic argument regularly prevails over the human values, not solely because politicians are enthralled by economists, but because the economist's dry statistics are often accompanied by a powerful threat—the company will close the factory if it doesn't get its way. If the standards are set too high, if the taxes are too onerous, the business enterprise will be shut down, destroying jobs and livelihoods. The threat is often bluff and artful exaggeration. In an earlier era, American industrialists warned that there would be economic chaos if children were prohibited from working in coal mines and garment factories.
>
> —Political reporter,
> William Greider [2]

The Patent That Wouldn't Fly

I know of no satisfaction," Herbert Hoover wrote in his memoirs, "equal to the growth under one's own hand of a great economic and human agency."[3] Hoover's "great economic and human agency" combined industry, scientific progress, and government to create an industry that helped win a world war and paved the way for the United State's economic power in the 21st century. Hoover was referring to his role in the "Golden Age of Aviation," the years between the world wars when the science of aerospace was transformed from a gentlemen's sport to a formidable economic and military armada.

Glenn E. Bugos, a history consultant for industry, describes the aerospace field as an economic phenomenon that has "consumed the major amount of research and development funds across many fields, subsidized innovation in a vast array of component technologies, evoked new forms of production, spurred construction of enormous manufacturing complexes, inspired technology-sensitive managerial techniques, supported dependent regional economies, and justified the deeper incursion of national governments into their economies."[4]

But at the beginning of World War I, the U.S. aerospace industry had produced less than a hundred aircraft, while France had produced 2,000 and Germany 1,000. Though the Wright brothers' breakthrough eleven years before had taken place through American ingenuity, the U.S. found itself far behind in the aerospace race. In fact, the entire aerospace enterprise was stalled and nearly floundered because of early patent infringement suits. The Wright brothers claimed in 1909 that nearly all airplanes being flown at that time, and for the duration of a patent, were an infringement on their own broadly defined airplane patent.[5]

If enforced, the Wright patent would have slowed, if not halted, the various engineering experiments that were being conducted by thousands of hobbyists, scientists, and entrepreneurs on the new invention. The issue bounced around the courts for years. Thankfully, the Wright brothers never got the all-powerful injunction against the groups and individuals exploring aviation while the patent remained in litigation. The issue was finally put to rest with the country's entry into World

War I. The U.S. government stepped in and forced a solution on the young industry and its patent problems: the Manufacturers Aircraft Association (MAA).

The MAA was patterned broadly after a similar association formed to deal with automobile patents around the turn of the century. The MAA, comprised of aeronautic industry leaders, created a patent pool. All aerospace firms, including the Wright brothers, shared key patents while paying into the pool without fear of infringement suits.[6] The MAA settled the earlier patent disputes and, by sharing its inventions with one another, the industry experienced a boost throughout World War I. The MAA, however, was not perfect in its composition. Critics saw it as composed mostly of industry insiders who were creating a patent monopoly that discouraged smaller companies and encouraged corruption. In order for the aerospace economy to really take off, the aerospace industries pushed for something that seems counter-intuitive to free-market ideas today: government regulation and policy.

By placing aerospace regulation under the Department of Commerce, Herbert Hoover "worked to provide the industry with economic and technical data designed to serve as the basis for better management decisions and better quality service," according to the historian David D. Lee.[7] By the end of the 1920s, the airline industry was producing 7,500 planes annually.[8] According to historian Roger Bilstein, "There seems to be a general consensus among aviation figures that the close of the twenties constituted an over-all benchmark of maturity in aeronautical development."[9]

Taxpayer support was an important, if not primary, impetus for aerospace's Golden Age. The industry was openly supported by an immense amount of taxpayers' money in two respects: The government became the aerospace industry's primary customer through military and postal service contracts and much of the basic scientific research on improving the technology was provided by government institutions. The government's National Advisory Committee for Aeronautics employed 6,000 researchers and owned $100 million in research equipment at the start of World War II.[10] As we know, the aerospace industry continues to profit from national research programs and military spending. As well, the industry remains under government regulation with little protest from aerospace companies.

The early aerospace industry shares striking similarities to the current biotechnology industry. Both, at their start, seemed to lack any real products. Airplanes, as yet unrealized by industry in their first ten years, were profitable only for wealthy playboys and circus-style daredevils. The amazing genetic discoveries have likewise failed to produce any significant products. Like the airplane, however, genetic discoveries hold much promise and may have a significant impact on our health and our lifestyles in a few years.

As was true of the aerospace industry, the government and people of the United States have a vested interest in a healthy and productive biotechnology industry, not only because it is an industry that we want to see as competitive but also because it promises public health benefits. For some patients, genetic research holds out the promise for life over death.

The patent problems of the biotechnology industry also appear similar to the early years of aerospace. Life patent claims on upstream knowledge threaten to stand in the way of true scientific advancement and, ultimately, will make the production of effective products impossible. As we will see, both the pharmaceutical companies and the biotechnology companies need to change their way of doing business in the next decade in order to survive. As was true with the first pioneers threatened by the Wright brothers' patent suit, the private and public explorations across the wide field of genetics will be hindered by patents that dam up basic science or by patents that are too broad.

There are at least two differences between those heady

days of aerospace innovation and the recent genomic revolution. First, the upstream knowledge came to be shared by all in the aerospace industry. This idea has yet to be embraced by the pharmaceutical and biotech companies. Second, the government, with an economic investment in the aerospace industry, needed to regulate the industry and police its commitment to the public good. So far, despite the millions of tax dollars that have been expended on biotechnology, the executive branch and Congress have maintained a "hands off" policy with regard to biotech innovation and patenting. The PTO claims it does not want to set policy while the courts struggle through thousands of patent infringement cases in an attempt to develop some ground rules.

The example of the airline industry also negates a common myth that is perpetrated by life patent advocates: An unregulated patent system is responsible for the current U.S. position as a world leader economically and technologically. While it might be proven that the United States is the world's economic and technological leader, this claim can hardly be attributed to the patent system. For the aerospace industry, patent protection on basic upstream knowledge had to be eliminated in order for innovation and industry to really occur. Throughout the history of the U.S., the patent system at times stimulated innovation but, at other times, it clearly hindered it and industry found itself in dire need of political intervention.

The patent system was hardly used during the first century of this country's existence, mostly covering agricultural devices. Around the turn of the 20th century, patents emerged as powerful and contentious tools for companies during the industrial revolution. But after 1930, patents were viewed again with the same suspicion held by the colonists of Jefferson's time. In 1938, President Franklin D. Roosevelt told Congress that patents were one of the causes of the "economic malaise gripping the country." Supreme Court Judge Learned Hand reflected the political and public sentiments of the time: "I think a great deal of the odium that has surrounded the subject is because patents are monopolies." Over the next few decades it became more and more difficult to be granted a patent, and yet technology flourished and the U.S. economy recovered from the worst depression the world had ever experienced.[11]

It was not until the 1970s and 1980s that the U.S. government's approach toward patents changed. Beginning in 1982, all appeals on patent litigations in the lower courts were brought to the Court of Appeals for the Federal Circuit (CAFC). CAFC immediately began delivering rulings that loosened the requirements for obtaining a patent. In its first five years, it overturned nearly 90% of lower court rulings that denied patents on the basis of being too "obvious."[12]

U.S. history contains many examples of technological and economic progress that were dependent on an atmosphere of cooperation between government, industry, and innovators that could only have been created *without* the current protection on intellectual property given by patents. Even intellectual property lawyers admit that the idea that patents spur innovation cannot be substantiated.

"Just as some people point to the number of patents to support the idea that the patent system produces more inventions, others can say that the standard of patentability is so low that the number of patents is meaningless and that few patents really are for true inventions," law professors Arthur R. Miller and Michael H. Davis write in a book for intellectual property students. "Clearly there is no basis for concluding that one theory is more 'effective' than the other or to make confident statements about what is the optimum amount of incentive to promote invention."[13]

In his book, *The Gene Hunters: Biotechnology and the Scramble for Seeds*, Casestous Juma writes that inventive innovation and economic development are less caused by patents and more a matter of a national attitude or policy toward supporting innovation:

It is difficult to establish a direct relationship between economic growth and patent activity, although patents are used as an indicator of innovation and economic development. Countries such as Japan have been able to make major advances in certain fields despite a relatively low rate of patent activity in those fields. What is important, though, is the capacity of a country to introduce inventions into the economic system. This issue is more a matter of the nature of the prevailing technology policy and does not necessarily relate to patents in a causal way.

Far from spurring innovation and economic development, life patents appear to be one of the causes of the biotechnology industry's recent financial slump. This chapter will look briefly at the future economic outlook of the biotechnology industry. It will look at the impact of genetic science on the development of new drugs and how both the biotechnology and pharmaceutical industries are revolutionizing their way of doing business. Like the dotcom industry, the biotechnology industry will fail if it does not produce real profits from real products. That goal, however, is seriously threatened by life patents. The financial future of both the pharmaceutical and biotechnology companies depends on the rejection of life patents. We will then look at the curious new "industry" of patent infringement cases. The billion-dollar patent infringement industry appears to do little more than swallow up money and resources that should be put toward scientific and economic progress. Lastly, an alternative to the patent system will be proposed that would reward biotech innovation, while getting us away from some of the injustices and pitfalls that life patents create in the fields of science, law, and economics.

Biotechnology: From Inventiveness to Industry

I want to emphasize that in our opinion, the question of whether patents should be made available for

"gene" inventions is not an issue that needs to be revisited. As I noted above, patents are an absolutely fundamental requirement for commercial success in our industry.
—Dennis J. Henner, Senior
Vice President of Research,
Genentech, Inc.[14]

As with the early aerospace industry, we are amazed and excited by the new discoveries in genetic research, but we have yet to see any successful products from that research. "Unfortunately, the deluge in data [in genomics] has yet to spur any dramatic increase in the number of new drugs discovered," *The Economist* commented in 2001.[15]

If biotechnology companies are to survive, they must make the jump from an era of inventiveness to an era of industry, producing real products that yield real profits. Those products will probably be in the form of drugs. Standing in the way of those drugs, however, is a minefield of life patents created by the biotech industry. As we have seen, life patents are destructive tools—exploiting indigenous cultures and endangering the world's seed and food supply—but their final victim may be the biotech industry itself.

A distinction needs to be made here between the pharmaceutical industry and the biotechnology industry, though that distinction is quickly being blurred. The pharmaceutical industry develops many drugs and therapies and has used patents to do so since the first medicinal patent in 1796.[16] With the exception of Amgen's Epogen, however, few of the drugs of the past decade were derived directly from patents on biological material. For the most part, drug patents have been and continue to be on chemical compounds that *affect* our biological functions, as opposed to life patents that patent the biological structures themselves. Unlike life patents, patents on drugs cover chemical compounds that, at least in theory, appear to have real utility, i.e., they ease headaches, fight pathogens, help us sleep, etc.

The pharmaceutical companies are coming off a good run.

In the past two decades, fuelled by so-called "blockbuster drugs," U.S. pharmaceutical companies have moved from sales of $22 billion to sales of $149 billion, giving back an average annual return of 25% to their investors.[17] By comparison, the average return for industrial companies is 6%.[18] Grocery stores have a profit margin of 1% or less. But experts say the days of the blockbusters are over and the old way of developing and marketing drugs is going to have to change.

The pharmaceutical companies has been doing business much like the Hollywood film industry. Just as the big film companies spend a great part of their money on producing a few expensive films a year in the hope of hitting a huge blockbuster, the drug companies have been sinking an ever increasing amount of money into research and development on a few drug targets in the hope of producing a small number of big blockbuster drugs. The large pharmaceutical companies have succeeded in this plan, in much the same way Hollywood has. They hit on drugs that treat common ailments—ulcers, high cholesterol, depression, arthritis, anemia—and therefore are able to make back their research and development costs because their market (the number of people with such ailments) is so large.

But there are fewer and fewer blockbuster drugs in the pharmaceutical companies' R&D pipeline, partly because the traditional way of discovering and developing drugs has gone about as far as it can in treating the big ailments. The future for the pharmaceutical industry, therefore, is in targeting a much wider range of ailments with much smaller market audiences. It means a "shift from a relative handful of blockbusters to a medical armamentarium consisting of thousands of sharpshooter drugs aimed at small disease populations," according to *Fortune* magazine.[19] In other words, the Hollywood model is being replaced with the independent film model or the "sharpshooter model:" A large number of drug products, each aimed at a much smaller group of people who will buy the drugs. In order to make this shift, the pharmaceutical companies are starting to dip into the advances of genetic research.

In contrast to the pharmaceutical industry, the biotech industry has yet to make a real profit.[20] A decade ago, the burgeoning biotech field was full of renegade scientists from universities and government programs pulling in millions of dollars in investments from venture capitalists. Stocks soared whenever they released their latest discoveries to the press, sometimes without publishing any scientific data to back up their claims. But after a decade of not bringing in much in the way of real revenue, the biotechnology industry has hit a catastrophic slump.

"Biotechnology has been through funding crises before, but almost everyone seems to agree that this is the worst one yet," a March 2003 *Economist* article states. "Capital to finance new ventures has pretty well dried up. Stockmarket flotations have stopped, and over the past three years the share prices of publicly quoted companies have declined so much that many firms are worth little more (and sometimes less) than the cash they have in the bank. Some are threatened with delisting."[21] A lead sentence in a May, 2002 *New York Times* article summed it up well: "It has been a horrendous year for the biotechnology industry."[22]

The reason the biotechnology industry is in trouble is because it has yet to make a real profit, and the reason it has not made a profit is because, as an industry, it has produced very few marketable products. In the words of John Wilderson of the investment company Galen Associates, "A biotech company is a pharma company without sales."[23]

Unlike the pharmaceutical industry, the biotechnology industry has not yet been able to produce drugs or therapies from their research.[24] For the most part, the industry has survived through announcements of its discoveries of upstream knowledge—and subsequent life patents on those discoveries—that buoyed stock prices and interested venture capitalists. Up until now, the biotechnology industry has been an industry of knowledge, producing maps of genomes and descriptions of genetic processes and structures. The industry has also developed genetic tests and genetic databases, but these knowledge-based products have very little use except in the context of further research on disease. The biotechnology industry has bought and traded this knowledge of human biological structures through the use of life patents. It has even made a little money by licensing and selling these patents to other researchers, and, in some cases, biotechnology companies have even profited from patent litigations. As exemplified disastrously by the dot-com industry, however, an industry cannot survive long without real products, real customers, and real profits.

Things are changing, however. The biotechnology companies, like the pharmaceutical companies, are going through what many economists call a revolution in their way of doing business. "The repercussions of genomics, in other words, are going to reach the furthest recesses of corporate constitution and culture," a recent report on the pharmaceutical industry by the Boston Consulting Group remarked. "A true revolution, in short—and one that is already well under way."[25]

Where once biotechnology companies were the golden boys of venture capitalists, some are now the "farm system" of the pharmaceuticals. Other biotech companies, like Amgen and Incyte Genomics, are starting to look like pharmaceutical companies themselves. "Our strategy now is to go all the way to becoming a fully integrated pharmaceutical company, not a database company," a science officer at Myriad said, reflecting the general trend.[26] Companies are buying up and merging with other biotechs and creating giant firms in which the primary goal is to develop drugs.[27]

An indication of this trend is the "release" of the dynamic geneticist Craig J. Venter by the company he created and presided over, Celera Genomics, early in 2002. Venter, an ex-NIH researcher, surprised the world in the early 90's by going private and challenging the U.S. government to a race to map the human genome. By all indications, Venter was "released" as the president of Celera because the company made the switch from concentrating on genome databasing to drug production.[28]

The future of both industries—the pharmaceutical companies shifting to sharpshooter drug development and biotechnology companies aiming for real products—lies in something called pharmacogenetics. Pharmacogenetics is the field of applying genetic technology to classic drug research and development.

In the entire history of the drug industry, only 500 disease targets—disease-causing functions in cells—have been researched. Because of the wealth of knowledge unearthed by genetic science, there are now 10,000 potential new disease targets. Experts claim that in order to turn these new targets into actual products, pharmaceutical companies must increase their R & D money as well as broaden their partnerships with smaller, more efficient research groups like biotechs and universities.[29] Again, genetic technological advancements will assist in this endeavor by streamlining the classic drug development process. While traditionally pharmaceutical companies developed drugs by trial and error on animals or humans, with pharmacogenetics computer models of specific molecular processes may be able to predict a drug's efficacy. Before ever having to test a drug on animals or humans, researchers may be able to predict a drug's side effects in the body and how the drug will interact with other drugs. Researchers may be able to customize the drug so that it can be effective on various individual body sensitivities.

What is the effect of life patents on this changing industry? When and if the new drugs promised by the genomic revolution reach the market, they will be covered not by life patents—patents that describe biological structures—but by patents that describe laboratory-produced chemical compounds that affect molecular structures. As we have seen, a life patent, basically a description of biological material, does not do anything by itself; it certainly does not "cure" the very gene, gene mutation, or protein that it might describe. If ever a drug is developed from studying the so-called "breast cancer" gene, then the drug company will apply for a patent on that drug, similar to the blockbuster drug patents that have always been allowed.

Ultimately, the promise of pharmacogenetics may not be scientifically possible. Though scientists may now have more drug targets, or more places to study how a disease moves through the body, this does not mean that they will come any closer to preventing or curing the disease. We heard similar promises of the possibility of conquering disease when advocates began pushing for the funding of the Human Genome Project. The Genome Project demonstrated that we have many more questions than we have answers about the human body. As well, the idea of customized drugs based on an individual's genetic profile sounds sexy, but it may not be realistically possible either scientifically or economically. The excitement around pharmacogenetics may be just another hype used in order to garner investors and maintain favorable public and political support for biotechnology.

That being said, we may never get to find out if pharmacogenetics is feasible if we continue to allow life patents to stand in the way of research. In order to study the 10,000 new disease-causing functions in cells, pharmaceutical companies, and the biotech and research institutes they employ, must be able to freely explore those cell functions. Pharmaceutical and biotechnology companies will not be able to develop thousands of new drugs with any efficiency if the basic descriptions of molecular materials are caught up in life patents. Exclusive licensing, royalty payments, and the suppression of research results in the name of life patents will all stand in the way of producing products. Patent litigations over basic knowledge will bankrupt the whole process before companies even start the long road of drug development.

The current situation in the biotechnology industry is

analogous to the threat that the aerospace industry was facing with the Wright brothers' patent infringement suits. Aerospace needed to make the move from an era of creative inventiveness to the creation of a real industry with products, profits, and a popular market. In order for efficient and useful airplanes to be developed, a broad number of inventions needed to be developed on top of the basic Wright design. In order to research the 10,000 drug targets, freedom must be given to the biotechnology industry to explore and improve upon the basic upstream knowledge.

We have seen many kinds of life patents in this book. Some, such as those covering genes or genomes found naturally, hardly meet the Patent Office's requirements and appear devastating to the progress of science. Others, such as those on genetically modified organisms, may meet the requirements but also cause negative impacts on innovation or even society. All life patents, however, stymie innovation in an industry that we would like to see survive. Like the early aerospace patents, we need to demand the regulation of some—mandating non-exclusive contracts, patent sharing, etc.—and get rid of the more harmful altogether.

The biotech and pharmaceutical companies have a lot of work to do to produce products from the genetic discoveries of the past twenty years. Tying that work up with life patents that lock in upstream knowledge will be like giving the Wright brothers a twenty-year monopoly on the airplane.

Patents vs. Marketing

The search for "magic bullets," the quest to discover and develop a viable drug, has traditionally been financially dangerous for drug companies. The main reason pharmaceutical companies historically demand broad patent protection is because of the enormous financial risk that companies undertake in bringing a drug to market. One in every hundred drug prospects makes it to market in traditional drug discovery and development. The cost for bringing a drug to market through the blockbuster method—including basic R & D, human trials, and FDA approval—is estimated by industry representatives to cost between $237 million and $780 million.[30]

The financial risk in bringing a blockbuster drug to market, however, is questioned by outsiders. The $237 million is an estimate made by the now-defunct Office of Technology Assessment in 1993, but it was calculated from information provided by industry representatives.[31] Critics such as James Love at the Center for Study of Responsive Law question what raw data was used to support those costs and if the cost includes initial research that was paid for by taxpayers. In fact, the OTA admits that they did not include tax credits. Love examined the tax breaks given to drug companies, especially the Orphan Drug Act, and found the cost of bringing a drug to market to be less than a third of what the OTA estimated, after taxes.[32] Love's data, culled from clinical trials at the NIH and the U.S. Treasury, "suggest industry reports of drug development costs may be biased or inflated, and that the taxpayer role in the development of Orphan Drugs is extensive."[33] Another impact on drug R & D, as we will see, is how much of the financial risk includes the cost of patent infringement cases.

The real corporate cost of bringing a drug to market is important because it reflects how important patents are to recouping research costs and, ultimately, to the financial success of a drug. If the cost of bringing a drug to market is only $100 million instead of $880 million then the importance of the patent is diminished.

Not surprisingly, new technology may make the cost and time needed to develop a drug even cheaper. The efficiencies in cost lie in the amazing progress that genetic research has made with their utilization of computers, robotics, and free public databases in developing drugs. With pharmacogenetics, researchers may be able to predict how the drugs affect our molecular structures before human trials have even begun. This will save thousands of hours of research by eliminating hopeless drugs in the beginning stages of research instead of during costly drug trials. When it comes to human trials, researchers may be able to hand pick the patients needed for the experience because they will have already modeled the type of patients they need.[34] According to a recent report by the Boston Consulting Group, pharmacogenetics may make the cost of developing a drug $300 million cheaper and take two years off the process.[35]

It is questionable whether patents on even downstream products—chemical compounds that make up the actual drugs—are really that important for a drug company's financial return. Although companies insist that the financial success of a drug is dependent on its patent protection, a drug's financial success appears to be more directly related to other factors. The OTA report concluded that profits did not change much between the time when a drug product was protected by a patent and when it was open to competition after a patent's expiration: "OTA analyzed changes in the U.S. market for 35 therapeutic compounds that lost patent protection from 1984 through 1987 and found that the sales decline is not nearly as steep as is commonly thought—at least not yet... Three years after patent expiration, the mean annual dollar sales of the original compound were 83% of mean sales revenue in the year of patent expiration." In other words, the profit made on a drug is about the same whether it is protected by a patent or not. A pharmaceutical industry publication on drug development echoed OTA's findings, admitting that "because many current drugs will lose patent protection relatively soon, patent concerns are relatively unimportant to their manufacturers."[36]

Why would the change in profit be so negligible between a drug that is protected by a patent and one that is not? The numbers seem to point to the primary reason for a drug product's success: marketing.

Bristol-Myers Squibb, the fifth largest prescription pharmaceutical company, spends $5.5 billion annually on advertising, marketing, selling, and administration, and only $1.9 billion on research and development.[37] GlaxoSmithKline, with drug revenues of more than $20 billion, has 40,000 employees in sales and marketing and 16,000 in research and development. Similar numbers are found in all the pharmaceutical companies. The contrast represents an economic decision to put the money where the company will get the greatest return. The priority is marketing and advertising, not research, even when the research is protected by patents.

The numbers imply that it is not at the patenting level where competitors are beaten, but at the marketing level. A huge marketing campaign will beat out competitors with similar products, especially the generic brands with much smaller marketing budgets.[38]

"Increasingly, big pharmaceutical companies are marketing-and-selling machines," *The Wall Street Journal* reported in 2001. "Having long outsourced basic science to academia and governmental organizations, they are now increasingly letting the biotechnology industry do the later-stage research and development. What Big Pharma has left is regiments of soldiers who drop free samples on offices, take doctors out to swanky dinners, and otherwise sing the praises of medicines that all too often have few benefits over rival products."[39]

Even when the product has dubious efficacy, drugs have been declared financial successes because of a well-moneyed marketing campaign. Thus we have the impressive marketing campaign for Claritin, the most profitable antihistamine in the history of medicine, even though only 46% of patients reported an improvement after taking the drug in clinical tests. Compare that with the 37% to 47% of patients that reported similar improvements after taking sugar pills (placebos) in the same clinical tests and one starts to understand the power of advertising.[40]

When the dubious importance of patents in gaining a return on R & D investment is weighed against the survival of the biotechnology industry, the need to eliminate life patents appears clear. Perhaps the industry is afraid to shake free of life patents because of the importance that patents have always been given with regard to classic chemical compound patents. Perhaps the upstart biotechnology companies a decade ago needed multiple patents to boost the confidence of their stockbrokers and investors. But those days are over. Both industries need to rethink their ways of doing business and remain extremely flexible over the next few years. Life patents will not give them that flexibility.

The $60 Billion Poison Pill: Patent Litigation

Building a [patent] portfolio requires enormous legal cost but contributes little to research incentives. Moreover, large firms (who are likely to have the larger patent portfolio, but not necessarily to be more creative) can use their portfolios to obtain royalties from their competitors and to restrict them to specific areas of technology.

—NIH Working Group[41]

I just wish these biotech companies would grow up.
—A major stockholder quoted during the
Amgen squabbles with Johnson & Johnson [42]

The 20,000 life patents that the patent office has granted on genetic material, and the 25,000 life patent applications that are pending, have often been compared to a minefield. It is an especially dangerous minefield because no one is quite sure just how many life patents there are or just what, exactly, they cover. It is also a fairly small minefield because there are only about 35,000 genes in the entire human genome. Over the next few years, researchers will be sifting through this minefield in order to research 10,000 new drug targets. Now imagine that researchers will be scurrying about this minefield knowing that the survival of their pharmaceutical or biotechnology company is at stake and one can begin to fathom the patent litigation warfare that will ensue.

A National Bureau of Economic Research study concluded: "The much higher litigation rate ... for the new area of biotechnology strongly suggests that the uncertainty associated with emerging technologies encourages litigation."[43] This uncertainty is caused by the broad requirements used by the patent office for awarding life patents that cover genetic material that researchers, as we have seen, have yet to precisely define. The patent office does not believe it is within its duties to examine how basic, broad, and upstream the knowledge is that a patent covers. They leave this to the courts. It has been left so much to the courts, in fact, that patent litigation itself might be considered an industry. But patent litigation only adds to the cost of bringing drugs to market, a cost that pharmaceutical and biotech companies cannot afford over the next few years.

In a survey of 530 biotech firms over a four-year period, six out of every one hundred patents were involved in patent litigation.[44] This means that, if all of the 25,000 life patents waiting in the patent office are approved, we can expect 1,500 litigations costing an average of $1.5 million a piece. That's a loss to companies of $2.25 billion dollars in the first four years of those patents' life. Another study reports that after patent litigation suits are reported in *The Wall Street Journal*, stocks for all companies involved in the litigation fall an average of 2%, translating to a median loss of $20 million. If we take the $20 million lost in stock by both companies, we have a net loss of $60 billion to all U.S. biotech and pharmaceutical companies before the cases are even decided.

Those numbers, however, are based on a survey that was taken in the early nineties, when the biotech industry was just revving up. Overall patent litigation has doubled in the years between 1991 and 2000.[45] Scientific progress in the life sciences also has an effect on the growing number of patent litigations. Patent litigation is predicted to increase now that we know humans have a significantly smaller number of genes than we thought when the Patent Office first started handing out life patents.[46] It's as if it was discovered that there was only so much land where one could find gold. The legal scrambling and scuffling will increase as the supply clearly does not meet the demand.

As of yet, obviously, the biotechnology industry as a whole has not collapsed under these enormous litigation costs. At last count, in early 2002, there were still about 1,400 companies in the U.S. who referred to themselves as biotech. However, as put so aptly by *The Economist*, many of these firms are "hanging on by their fingertips" and may soon "drop off the cliff."[47] The enormity of litigation costs are an increasingly large threat to smaller biotechnology firms especially, and, given its precarious financial state, to the whole industry at large.

If you're playing penny poker and all your friends show up with five dollars in pennies, you can play for hours and maybe even walk home with about the same amount of money. But if one of your friends shows up with fifty dollars in pennies, then he can raise the ante and the stakes such that you will lose quite quickly.

This is what happens in patent litigation. The companies with the most money—the ones that can withstand long and expensive lawsuits—will win the game. The ante—a preliminary injunction by a large company—may sink a small biotech company that depends on its few patents to stay financially afloat. At this point, without ever going to trial to see if the big company has a case, the smaller company may settle the case by working out a licensing agreement. In fact, this is exactly what happens. A 1996 study showed that "financially strong firms use preliminary injunctive relief to prey upon weaker firms by driving up their costs."[48] The reaction by smaller R & D firms (in all sectors) is obvious. Concerns about patent litigation is the major factor in "deciding to pursue an innovation" for over half of smaller firms, but is a major factor for only a third of larger companies, another study affirms.[49]

In his book, *The Patent Wars*, Fred Warshofsky recounts the story of early biotech innovator Professor Donald Comb whose laboratory began producing Taq DNA polymerase in 1987. Taq DNA polymerase is an enzyme that serves to make copies of DNA molecules over the course of few hours and is used in almost all gene research projects. The enzyme, and the process in which it functions, was well known to researchers for over a decade and was explicated in scientific journals since the 1970s. Nevertheless, a biotech company called Cetus Corporation was granted a patent on Taq DNA polymerase because it had correctly measured the molecular weight of the enzyme. Comb "considered his options," according to Warshofsky, "a product already in production and possible sales of $500,000 a year versus a couple of million on fighting a patent infringement suit with a decidedly uncertain outcome. He chose the former and shut down his polymerase production line."[50]

The idea that patent lawsuits may be a deterrent to scientific innovation is, in itself, a reversal of the original intent of the patent system. The fact that these lawsuits are used against smaller firms and their innovations in particular is especially disheartening. Many of the great breakthroughs, in biotechnology as well as in the entire history of scientific discoveries, were made by individuals or small companies. Big companies may be good for turning these discoveries into products and marketing them, but the creativity comes from the men and women unbridled by corporate bureaucracies and bottom-line requirements. Once again, we have only to look at the Wright brothers as an example.

Patent litigation appears to hurt all involved. It certainly doesn't help the taxpayers, who have to pay the judges, provide for the jurors, and the upkeep of the courtroom. It doesn't help the U.S. economy, especially when the litigation is most often between two American companies. Studies show that U.S. companies are involved in patent litigation five times more than foreign firms.[51] It doesn't help scientific progress because it stalls any progress by any side as long as it remains in court. A number of life-saving biotech discoveries may be kept from the public for months as litigation drags on. It doesn't help stockholders in the companies. It never helps the loser of the patent battle, whether that loser is the one with the original patent or the one who is accused of infringing on it. Finally, it seldom helps the winner because of the time and money that was expended on the trial.

But not everyone loses. Intellectual property lawyers make money, whether they're on the losing side or the winning. Attorneys Gerald Hosier and Raymond Niro have each made over $400 million from patent litigation cases.[52] Other lawyers charge up to 45% contingency fees.

An assortment of other companies are popping up to reap the profits of patent litigation. Corporate executives complain about the "patent trolls," companies that buy up patents with the intention of making their entire profit on patent litigation. In a series of articles in *The Reporter* in the summer of 2001, writer Brenda Sandburg reported, "In the last decade, patent enforcement has grown into a multibillion dollar shadow industry that is transforming America's patent system from a security fence protecting inventors from exploitation into a money-minting machine for a few patent holders." Other companies have been created to sell patent enforcement insurance industry. People can even invest in ownership of patents through certain brokers solely for the purpose of making money from lawsuits.[53] It's a virulent evolution that parallels the rise of drug resistant superbugs. Like the superbugs, litigation looks to be on the verge of spinning out of control.

Patent litigation is, frankly, an industry that the U.S. economy can do without. It saps money and human resources away from what the biotechnology industry should be doing: exploring the human body with the hopes of fighting disease. Patent infringement is an illusionary industry, maintained by the continued granting of life patents. It fails not only the public good, but the U.S. economy in general.

As American as Swiss Army Knives

But, say many, strong legal protection for life patents is in the best interest of the U.S. economy. According to this myth, the patent system protects the investment of U.S. companies and investors in new technologies. Without life patents, U.S. companies would not invest in biotechnology or drug research. If companies and investors did not invest, then an important sector of the U.S. industry would decline and negatively impact the whole U.S. economy.

This may have held some truth twenty years ago, but the world economy has changed such that the U.S. patent system no longer protects the U.S. economy and its citizens' inventiveness. It is very true, as the myth supposes, that the biotech and pharmaceutical industries are worried about their investments and financial future. But whether they are worried about the *United States'* biotech industry and financial future is a different story.

Already, in 1996, 46% of the total patents awarded by the U.S. Patent Office were awarded to foreign inventors or companies.[54] Despite the belief that the U.S. has the most innovative medical research in the world, the United Kingdom retains the most patents worldwide on drugs, medicines, and biotechnology.[55]

The truth is, many of the companies pushing for internationally enforced life patents are multinational corporations. Multinational, in a sense, means that the companies do not owe their allegiances to any country, only to themselves. U.S. citizens may sit on the board, or work on the staff, or vote as stockholders, but the decisions of multinational companies are not based on how well America is doing economically or how many Americans are employed by the companies. Their decisions are based on how well the company alone is doing.

In 1971, there were 280 American-based corporations on a list of the world's 500 largest multinationals. Thirty years later, that list has dwindled to 157.[56] Although biotechnology companies in the United States are, for the most part, still U.S. companies, the pharmaceutical partners who will ultimately profit from biotech discoveries are increasingly not American. Four of the top ten pharmaceutical companies are foreign-based companies.[57] Of the top agrochemical companies, Syngenta is a Swiss company, Aventis is based in France. The pharmaceutical and biotechnology industries are quickly becoming global industries that are placing their research, factories, and corporate offices in countries where labor is cheap, technology is available, and taxes are low.

Correspondingly, an increasingly global U.S. patent system has a negative impact on both American technology and the American workforce when it comes to the biotechnology industry. First, foreign-owned drug and biotech companies are directly profiting from both public and private U.S. research by basing more and more of their R & D in the United States. These companies do not come to the United States to employ expensive American workers; they come to make use of emerging U.S. technologies. Fifty percent of the drug research and development in the U.S. is paid for by foreign companies. In 1992, there were 250 foreign-owned research facilities in the United States. That number has grown to 715.[58]

Second, U.S. companies are basing more and more of their R & D overseas because, as in other industries, the workforce is cheaper elsewhere. In the past twenty years, we have seen the factories of the automobile, aerospace, and textile industries leave the U.S. for cheaper labor. The movement is now starting to affect white collar laborers such as engineers and middle managers. American-based companies have expanded their research and development overseas to $14 billion, triple what it was in 1986.[59] If a company can hire 20 Korean geneticists for the price of one U.S. geneticist, then it will do it.

In order to maximize profits, companies cannot afford to care about the jobs that are lost in the U.S., they cannot afford to care about the technology that may leave the country, and they cannot afford to worry about whether the U.S. has a healthy biotechnology or pharmaceutical industry. In the age of globalization, all they can care about is whether their biotech or pharmaceutical company is doing well. William Greider, in this book *One World Ready or Not*, explains that "financial investors monitor and punish corporations or even entire regions of the globe if these places appear to be creating impediments to profitable enterprise or unpleasant surprises for capital. If this sounds dictatorial, the global financiers also adhere to their own rough version of egalitarian values: they will turn on anyone, even their own home country's industry and government, if the defense of free capital seems to require it."[60]

In fact, the only reason a multinational corporation and its investors might worry about the U.S. economy is that the U.S. still provides the best place to market and sell products. In other words, multinationals want the technology developed with U.S. tax dollars and they want U.S. consumers who will buy back that technology in the form of a product.

The majority of basic research being done in start-up biotech companies and universities still takes place in the United States. But the economics of globalization are quickly infiltrating every industry in the world. Already, many of these universities and biotechnology companies have contracts with large pharmaceuticals and agrochemical corporations that have no connection to the U.S. economy. And more and more, patents on life will be owned by a group of shareholders with no national ties. The idea that life patents protect American inventors and investors and stimulate the national economy has no statistical basis.

Jefferson, the father of the U.S. patent system, would take offense at the fact that his system is being used to give multinational companies control over American technologies. It is as if we are selling the resources of the United States and then having to buy them back at inflated prices as products. In fact, isn't that precisely the situation that culminated in our Revolutionary War?

Yes, and in response to corporations with monopolies on tea and a British government that abused patents, our forefathers created a document that would protect their new government from similar abuses. That document, the Constitution, does not make patents a right, rather it mandates that the government promote "the progress of science and useful arts, by securing for limited times to authors and inventors the exclusive right to their respective writings and discoveries." The idea was to balance private interests with public good. Patents on life fail at this basic Constitutional mandate.

So do we have to start dumping boxes of pills from Swiss drug companies into the Boston Harbor? No, we must merely get back to protections the Constitution offered to inventors and society in the first place.

CHAPTER SIX

Twisting the Constitution

> Congress shall have the power... To promote the progress of science and useful arts, by securing for limited times to authors and inventors the exclusive right to their respective writings and discoveries.
>
> —U.S. Constitution

Jefferson and the Hot Issue of 1791

Thomas Jefferson probably would have loved the genomic revolution. As a farmer who enjoyed experimenting with plants and different breeds of animals, he was fascinated with the natural sciences. Jefferson's farm at Monticello became a living laboratory where he cultivated over 250 varieties of edible plants and an estimated 150 different varieties of fruit.[1] Doubtless, many of the most recent genetic discoveries would have fascinated him.

Jefferson was also interested in patents. It was his job to be interested. As the first Secretary of State, Jefferson was put in charge of reading and approving the first patent applications for the newly formed United States. As a reflection of the importance that he gave to patents, Jefferson only granted three patents the first year he took the position. Of the 114 patent applications that were considered seriously during the first two years of the Patent Office, only 49 were granted.[2]

Jefferson also read and reviewed each patent that came in. Further, the Secretary of War and the Attorney General assisted him in reviewing them as well.[3] In some cases, Jefferson personally tested the proposed inventions.

Jefferson's caution with patents reflected the discussions and worries of the day. The general public understood patents to be very political matters. Many were suspect of co-opting a system of patents that resembled the British model where the crown used patents to monopolize whole industries and fill its own coffers. During the 17th century, the British crown had restrictive patent monopolies on such basic materials as salt, oils, vinegar, and starch. A proposed fee that would be levied on land patents in America precipitated in the "Pistole Fee" controversy in Virginia in the 1750s and added to the rumblings about unfair taxation that led to the Revolutionary War. In fact, the Constitution of the United States does not contain the word "patent" at all because the word would have reminded too many people of the monopolistic inequities caused by the British system.

Jefferson, too, was concerned with the threat of economic monopolies being created by powerful individuals. In fact, Jefferson was initially quite nervous about awarding patents at all because of this threat.

Jefferson wrote a letter to James Madison in which he questioned whether the protection given by a patent—at that time fourteen years was proposed—had any benefit. "The saying that there shall be no monopolies, lessens the incitements to ingenuity, which is spurred on by the hope of a monopoly for a limited time, as of fourteen years; but the benefit of even limited monopolies is too doubtful, to be opposed to that of their general suppression."[4]

In the letter, Jefferson hoped that a bill of rights would soon be added to the Constitution, and that in this document the abolishment of monopolies would become law: "It is better to establish trials by jury, the right of habeas corpus, freedom of the press and freedom of religion, in all cases, and to abolish standing armies in time of peace, and monopolies in all cases than not to do it in any. The few cases wherein these things may do evil, cannot be weighed against the multitude wherein the want of them will do evil."[5]

Thomas Jefferson, farmer, lawyer, diplomat, and states-man, was also an inventor. Among other things, Jefferson invented the revolving chair ("a whirl-i-gig" his critics called it), a folding chair (he brought it along to church when seating was scarce); a light buggy to be pulled by horse, a pedometer, and, his most famous invention, a modernized plough. But although Thomas Jefferson is considered the Father of the Patent Office, he never applied for a patent. He wanted his ideas to be put into the public domain, to be improved upon and studied, but he did not believe the patent system was the best vehicle for this.

Jefferson hoped that one of his inventions, a "hemp-break" that is used to break up the stalks of the hemp plant, would be helpful to farmers. "(A)s soon as I can speak of [the hemp-break's] effect with certainty," Jefferson said, "I shall describe it anonymously in the public papers, in order to forestall the pre-vention of its use by some interloping patentee."[6] Over two hundred years later, the U.S. government's genome project still follows that practice of Jefferson's—public release of its disclo-sures within twenty-four hours. The reasoning is much the same: fear of an "interloping patentee" who might monopolize the information.

Benjamin Franklin is another founding father who is well known as a prolific inventor—and he, too, didn't believe intel-lectual protection on his inventions would promote the progress of science. Despite having invented bifocals, the lightning rod, the Franklin stove, and many other things, Franklin never applied for a patent. Franklin wanted to publish his ideas quick-ly, so that they could be put to use by whoever saw them as valu-able. "Gov'r Thomas was so pleas'd with the construction of this stove," Franklin wrote about his stove, "that he offered to give me a patent for the sole vending of them for a term of years; but I declin't it from a principle which has ever weighed with me on such occasions, viz., that, as we enjoy great advantages from the inventions of others, we should be glad of an opportunity to serve others by any invention of ours; and we should do freely and generously."[7]

Jefferson's suspicions about patents are important today because the monopolies he worried about are emerging through life patents. Ironically, Jefferson is often referred to when proponents of life patents want to defend their position. The legal precedent he started in the patent office was cited in *Diamond v. Chakrabarty*. But it is doubtful whether Jefferson would have supported the expansion of patent policy to cover life forms and molecular biology.

The concerns of Franklin and Jefferson cover real inventions, things conceived of and created by the human hand. But Jefferson also recognized that patents covered ideas and he feared the monopolies that patents might give in that context as well. "No matter what form monopolies took, Jefferson considered them an affront to the teaching of nature, nowhere more than in the case of monopolies in the form of patent rights," historian Charles A. Miller writes in *Jefferson and Nature: An Interpretation*. "He thought that ideas, formulas, and the physical properties of materials were all part of nature and were therefore no more the legitimate subject of private property than was the sea or unworked land. Although the capacities of physical nature might be discovered, nobody invented them." [8]

Since the founding of the Patent Office, the context of patents has changed dramatically within science, technology and commerce, but Jefferson's warnings about monopolies hold true today more than ever.

The Game of Stem Cell Monopoly

Anyone who has ever played and lost the game of Monopoly knows the frustration that comes when one player has bought up all the property and is charging exorbitant rent.

Nothing is worse than staring ahead at the next twelve spaces and seeing a row of someone else's hotels. One cannot move without fear of landing on an owned property and being hit with a fee.

In the summer of 2001, President George W. Bush announced his decision that federal funds would only be allowed for research on the 60 or so embryonic stem cell lines that were already in existence. The declaration triggered a national debate on stem cells that involved scientists, ethicists, and ordinary citizens. Buried among the political, scientific, and moral arguments for and against Bush's decision was an incredible discovery: All stem cell lines—those existing and any yet to be developed—were controlled by one company under one patent.[9]

A researcher at the University of Wisconsin, Dr. James A. Thomson, originally isolated human embryonic stem cells in 1998 and was awarded the patent. The patent, described as "iron clad" by an attorney who drafted it, covers both the patent for isolating embryonic stem cells and the stem cell lines derived from these.[10] The patent was handed over to the university's research foundation that in turn gave exclusive proprietary rights to a California company, Geron Corporation. In essence, the patent gave Geron the right to restrict all stem cell research and demand royalties and ownership of all products developed from stem cell lines.

Like the loser of a game of monopoly, stem cell researchers found they could not move forward at all because the whole board was owned by Geron. It was estimated that up to 50% of the federal money that went into researching stem cells would go to licensing fees for the patent.[11] Legal experts thought that some overseas owners of stem cells were afraid to come forward, fearing patent infringement suits by Geron.[12]

"The only way to go in this area is to allow scientists unlimited access to these cell lines," Robert Goldman, professor of cell and molecular biology at Northwestern University, told

The Chicago Tribune. "There should be no restrictions, no tied hands, no reporting to the University of Wisconsin, no worries about patent infringement. I think it's terrible the way the whole thing has worked out."[13]

"Doesn't it seem unfair," Kent College law professor Lori Andrews wrote in an editorial for *Newsday.com*, "that our tax dollars will be used to support research that will benefit the small number of cell line owners, who will then be able to charge us whatever they want to use resulting products?"[14]

President Bush stated in his speech that there were as many as 60 stem cell lines in existence throughout the world. For many life scientists, this was a surprisingly large number. Once again, the race for patents on research results engendered an atmosphere of secrecy. The various universities and institutes working on stem cell lines—supported by contracts with biotech and pharmaceutical companies—had been hiding their research for years and protecting it with lawyers and contracts.

Some politicians and researchers were afraid that there would soon be a "brain drain" after Bush's announcement and the discovery of the University of Wisconsin patent. They feared stem cell scientists would leave the United States for research environments overseas that would not be hindered by patent and government interference. "Researchers in other countries have a double advantage," Rebecca S. Eisenberg, a biotechnology and patent law expert, told *The New York Times*.[15] Not only did the president limit research to 60 stem cells, but the United States is the only country where a patent on stem cells existed.

With the exception of one type of stem cell found in bone marrow, stem cell research has yet to produce any products. In fact, in a few years, scientists may find that stem cell research is a dead end. In his speech, President Bush warned that stem cell research may go the way of fetal tissue research: an exciting prospect that has produced nothing but disastrous results. Much of the optimism about stem cell therapy may be wishful thinking boosted by biotech companies looking to impress stock-holders.

Nevertheless, even getting to the point of discovering that stem cells lead to a scientific dead end may be hindered by proprietary rights. Researchers in this country may not be able to pass Go. Indeed, a brain drain on stem cell researchers may have to occur in order for the researchers to avoid infringing on the stem cell patent.

Within days of the president's speech, the University of Wisconsin research foundation that had originally licensed their patent out to Geron brought a lawsuit against the company in order to loosen its monopoly on stem cells. "Through this action," Carl Gulbrandsen, the managing director of the foundation, said, "we hope to enable more academic researchers and private companies to join the search for new therapies and cures for some of the world's most debilitating diseases."[16]

The lawsuit was settled with Geron agreeing to relinquish most of its exclusive rights to the patent. Yet the patent remains in the hands of one organization, the University of Wisconsin.[17] Though they have promised that they will share the stem cells with other researchers, the university still retains the exclusive right to license all stem cell lines.

When Dr. Thomson applied for his patent, stem cell research was a small field confined to obtuse articles in scientific journals. Three years later, it exploded on our newspapers' front pages with promises of therapies for leukemia, Alzheimer's disease, and a long list of other diseases and ailments. This experience suggests that seemingly unimportant biological material today may become the springboard for life-saving technologies tomorrow. When we award patents on biological material that we still know so little about, we may be setting up unforeseen monopolies on important medical technology. To claim ownership on biological material now is to shut down the roads of medical progress in the future.

It is a system that embodies Jefferson's worst fears.

The Unconstitutional Game of Patent Monopoly

Briefly, then, let us note how allowing patents on life goes against the Constitutional intent behind the patent system. The Constitution mandates the government to:

- **Promote the progress of science**: We have seen how life patents on upstream knowledge have clearly slowed the progress of the life sciences and medicine. Although the Wright brothers' airplane may have been a unique breakthrough, the aerospace industry—including the Wright brothers—would not have progressed at all if the original invention had been constrained by patents. The same is true of patents on upstream knowledge.

- **Promote the useful arts**: "Useful arts" implies a concern with public good; i.e. a mandate to examine if the invention assists in the public's health or well-being. As we have seen, individuals and groups have been negatively affected by life patents, on many different levels. A "useful art" does not take away the very rights the Constitution outlines. Nor should "useful arts" risk ecological destruction or the termination of crops, as some of the inventions covered by life patents threaten to do.

- **Secure for limited times to authors and inventors the exclusive right to their respective writings and discoveries.** Those that have made the discoveries in genetic science are not getting rewarded for their work through life patents. Most of the discoveries in molecular biology are built on years of cooperative research between many different groups and individual scientists. Some discoveries, such as the BRCA gene and CCR5, can be traced to very specific groups that did the major leg work, but, as we have seen, they are not getting the credit for their work with patents. The patents, instead, are going to companies who may have done some work on the discovery, but have been awarded the patent because of luck or a powerful legal team. Other life patents, such as quinoa and Indian neem, are little more than blatant rip-offs from cultures whose history has long demonstrated the "utility" of such inventions and refutes the "inventiveness" claimed in patents.

The search for knowledge is a noble goal. Science is a human endeavor that should be encouraged. But the issue of life patents is not the same as science. Patenting is about property rights. As property rights, the public good must be considered.

Public Good and Property

"The U.S. Congress, after hearings, reported that in their view, 'the patent law is not the place to exercise moral judgments about scientific activity'. This continues to be the well accepted attitude of the USA," Ronald Schapira, a U.S. patent attorney, told an international conference on patents and morality. "If biotechnology and its inventions are to be regulated in the US, it is not the function of the patent lawyers or the Patent Office to do so... In my view, patent offices and patent examiners generally do not have sufficient expertise or qualifications to judge morality or even societal risks of inventions, particularly biotechnology inventions."[18]

The U.S. Patent Office says that it does not want to take an ethical stand on the life patent issue. But the decision to distance itself from the human consequences of its actions *is* an ethical position. The U.S. Patent Office says it is not its job to decide or shape policy. But it is shaping policy by allowing life patents. By treating biological materials and knowledge as commodities, the Patent Office is forming policy domestically and internationally.

Allowing life forms and genes to be patented has all the appearances of a law, but it is not. As we recall, the judges saw their decision in *Chakrabarty* as a question of patentability; i.e. whether Chakrabarty's invention met the requirements of the Patent Office. They did not view their decision as a question of whether, ultimately, life forms and genes should be patentable.

It was a legal circle game in which no decision was actually made: The Court based its decision on Patent Office require-ments, the Patent Office based its policy of awarding life patents on the Supreme Court decision. And the Supreme Court point-ed out that it was not making law on whether life forms should be patentable. It wanted to leave that, the real decision, up to Congress. Congress never made any decision.

And so, no decision has really been made. Life patents are a product of bureaucratic inertia, if anything, with large pushes from the biotechnology industry. But their continued existence not only goes against the original intent of patenting, but also repeat-edly offends the personal rights of individuals and communities.

At their root, patents are property rights—they are called *intellectual* property rights. The general idea is that property rights protect the owners of the property, which, in fact, they do. But property rights, as they were understood by Jefferson and the founders of this country, also protect others with property and even those that do not have property. Harvard Law Professor Joseph Singer writes, "The law has... always imposed obligations on owners to use their property with a view toward protecting other owners and the legitimate interests of the community."[19]

All property laws, like all rules, are shaped by moral and ethical decisions. Property laws are a government's decision on where the line is between personal freedom and the good of society. Where that line lies is an ethical choice and is based upon a community's cultural or political viewpoint. In socialist countries, individual property is judged as being less important than communal or state property. In a pure socialist state, an individual cannot claim land as property. The United States takes a more "liberal" view, in that a person can own property (if legally gained) and can do more or less what they want with that property.

But even the most liberal property laws that have the least amount of government interference with an individual's prop-erty rights weigh those rights against the good of the community. Take the most common definition of property: physical land that you own. In any community in the United States, the freedom you have with your land is limited by multiple zoning laws and environmental constraints, as well as any number of criminal laws. In most communities there are restrictions on the size and number of buildings you can put on the property, the kind of occupants (commercial or residential), the number of residents, the nature of the business, the number and kinds of roads, and the amount of land that can be cleared. In many towns, even the colors you can paint your house is limited by city government. These "freedom limiting" laws are moral judgments made by the government on where the line is between freedom of the individual and the good of the community.

What are the goods of the community that are being weighed against your desire to build a neon pink machine-gun factory on a half-acre of land? The economic good of the community is important; i.e. your neighbors want to maintain the value of their homes and your ill-colored factory might detract from that. As well, the cost to city services may affect everyone's property taxes. More importantly, however, are health and safety issues: Traffic on the two-lane road in front of your land will increase to a dangerous level and the factory may take away limited water, sewage, and electricity from the rest of the community. The run-off from your factory may affect your neighbors' gardens or even the community's water source. The billowing smoke may have an environmental effect as well as an effect on health. Questions of safety may be raised about the production of machine guns within 500 feet of the neighborhood high school.

Property laws weigh the good of the community—most importantly with regard to health and safety—against the rights of an individual or an individual corporation. Regardless of how you or I may profit from a pink machine gun factory, or a corporation may profit from Bolivian quinoa or the human genes of Tristan de Cunha, the good of the community must be weighed.

The Patent Office's policy of awarding property rights on biological material is analogous to handing out parcels of public land with no restrictions on how that land will be used. Outside comments on patents applications are certainly not allowed. The only parties involved with the application process are the patent office and the company or person who applies for the patents. No third parties have any say, even if a third party is directly affected by the patent or the patent covers its biological material. There is nothing in the process of granting life patents that allows for consideration of the good of the affected community. But with things as universal as human genes and important as the world's food source, the affected community includes all of us.

The question we should be asking ourselves is why do we have laws that limit the colors we can paint our houses but our laws do not keep corporations from using their patented property to slow scientific progress? Why do our property laws keep us from making money by building a machine gun factory but do not keep biotech companies from exploiting developing countries and stealing their genetic heritage through patents? Why do we have laws that protect our community from health hazards, but do not have controls that might protect our food sources? Why do we demand protection and access to public parks and shared space, but allow patents that restrict access to basic knowledge about human and plant biology?

We cannot accept the answer "because it's the law."

While Schapira and others may be correct in stating that the Patent Office's 190 Ph.D.'s in its biotechnology department are not qualified to make ethical decisions about the patents they are awarding, the question remains, then who is? The final chapter attempts to answer that question.

CHAPTER SEVEN

Patenting Humans and Beyond

Who Decides Our Future?

> Just as war is too important to leave to the generals,
> science and technology are too important to leave in the
> hands of the experts.
>
> —Sheldon Rampton and
> John Stauber from
> *Trust Us, We're Experts.*[1]

Patenting Humans

In April 2001, a patent that covers a particular process for producing cloned mammals was issued to the University of Missouri. Unlike other patents issued to research institutions and biotechnology companies that are used to boost investor confidence, this patent attracted little attention. Press releases were not issued, the university did not announce millions of dollars for its licensing, and scientists and businessmen did not grab the microphone and describe their successful "invention."

Nearly one year later, a Washington think tank, the International Center for Technology Assessment (ICTA), discovered the patent and sounded an alarm. The patent clearly covered the cloning of all mammals, *including humans.* Critics analyzed the patent and discovered that the lawyers who had drawn up the patent deliberately mention human cells in the patent in order to cover human cloning.[2]

Richard Warburg, a patent lawyer for the animal cloning company Infigen, told *The New York Times*, "It definitely is a patent for cloning a human, and under the laws we have right now, it might actually cover the human."[3]

"It is horrendous that we could define all of human life as biological machines that can be cloned, manufactured, and patented," Andrew Kimbrell, Executive Director of ICTA, said in response to the patent.[4]

By granting the cloning patent, the Patent Office bypassed national discussions on human cloning and initiated its own policy on the technology for the United States. In fact, at the time of the ICTA's discovery of the patent in spring of 2002, Congress had been hotly debating the human cloning issue for months. The patenting process was used to control an issue and make policy on a controversy that had yet to be decided democratically.

Coincidentally, the European Union found itself in a similar situation two years earlier. In February 2000, Greenpeace discovered a patent granted by the European Patent Office that covered the cloning of human embryos. Within a month of Greenpeace's discovery, a horrified European Parliament voted to oppose the patent. The European Patent Office immediately admitted that granting the patent had been a mistake.[5]

The U.S. is faced with the parallel situation of the University of Missouri's patent on human cloning. Yet neither Congress nor the Executive branch has issued any substantive response.

The case demonstrates that the Patent Office has already moved into the arena of granting property rights over entire human bodies. By allowing a patent on cloning and clones, the Patent Office is allowing a patent on a scientifically manipulated human birth and all of its products; i.e. human beings. Although cloning technology has not been developed to the extent that scientists can produce human clones—and it is questionable whether it ever shall[6]—the University of Missouri patent demonstrates the extent to which the Patent Office has been allowed to act on its own without democratic debate.

The idea of patenting plants or animals may have been incredulous to many people just a few decades ago. Likewise, the idea of patenting a human being was a laughable concept a few years ago. In the late 1990s, activists Jeremy Rifkin and Stuart Newman applied for a patent on a theoretical part-human, part-animal hybrid. Although such a creature is still technologically impossible, they wanted to challenge the Patent Office, and the public, to consider the "slippery slope" of life patents. If the Patent Office and the courts allow patents on genetically manipulated mammals and human genes, why not a human with animal genes or vice versa? The two hoped that the patent would end up in court so that policy could be made concerning how "human" something had to be in order to be patentable. The patent was flatly rejected in 1999 on the grounds that although other mammals and animals could be patented, a human could not.

Biotechnology companies, and the public at large, took little notice of Newman's and Rifkin's activity.[7] At the time, many thought that the Patent Office was clear on not awarding patents on humans and, furthermore, did not see it as a goal of biotechnology companies. "This is a somewhat academic subject," patent lawyer Tom Ciotti with Morrison & Foerster said at the time. "We haven't been claiming things like that [in patent applications.]"[8]

All that seems to have changed.

With the University of Missouri's human cloning patent, we have suddenly found ourselves at the bottom of Newman's and Rifkin's slippery slope. In the years between Rifkin and Newman's patent application and the University of Missouri's clone patent, the Patent Office has broadened intellectual property rights to include humans with no involvement from the courts or from Congress. While our legislatures debate the morality of cloning humans, the Patent Office is already handing out patents on them.

The University of Missouri promised that it will not use its patent to explore human cloning: "We have absolutely no interest in using this to research humans and we will not license this technology to anyone for use in humans," Christian Basi, a spokesman for the University of Missouri told *The New York Times*. "This *gives us control* of this particular technology so we will know that this technology will not be used in humans."[9] The striking element in Basi's statement is the acknowledgement that the university does indeed have control of this process of human cloning and has the power to decide who gets to use it and how. Human cloning is not in the hands of a democratically elected government, but in the hands of a private organization.

The university may, indeed, have no interest in human cloning, but what of its corporate partners? And how much control does the university really have controlling the ultimate use of its patent, especially through complex licensing agreements that involve many groups? When the patent was awarded, a Massachusetts company called Biotransplant Inc. was in partnership with the university, but Biotransplant's main business was licensing technology to third-party businesses. Did the university oversee the agreements Biotransplant involved itself in?

Biotransplant had also hoped to develop a business from xenotransplantation, the transplanting of animal organs into human beings. Early in 2003, however, Biotransplant declared bankruptcy.[10] The human cloning patent is again for sale.

On the other hand, the monopoly control that life patents provide could be used by those who want to see specific genetic research stopped or used for purely ideological reasons. As we have seen, life patents slow scientific innovation because patent holders are given monopolies on large segments of research. But a scenario can also be envisioned whereby life patents may be utilized by religious or political groups in order to control or halt particular studies on human biology. A patent on human cloning might be particularly attractive to such groups. Fringe political or ideological groups are already attempting to use genetic science and biotechnology toward their own political or religious ends. A religious group called the Raelians made head-lines in early 2003 when it claimed to have cloned a human and was planning on cloning many more. The Raelians did not apply for a patent (in fact, such a patent may infringe on the University of Missouri's patent), but such a scenario is not far off. Whether one thinks that we should explore human cloning or not, the idea of seeding control of such controversial tech-nology to a single organization—perhaps simply to the highest bidder—is a frightening prospect.

National policy has been formed within the narrow focus of the Patent Office without any input from the public or even the politicians that are supposed to represent them. While we debate, the patent office decides…

Downright Un-American

To judge from some of the rhetoric, the idea that the pub-lic good or ethics should be considered in patent policy is some-times deemed equivalent to attacking the American way of life. Robert M. Goldberg, a senior fellow at the Manhattan Institute, seemed to imply this in an editorial in *National Review*. Goldberg wrote the article in response to South Africa's deci-sion to override patent protections on AIDS drugs and the Bush administration's similar consideration concerning Cipro during the anthrax attacks. "The assault on patents as a public-health policy turns out to be mere camouflage for an attack on capital-ism," Goldberg wrote. "To the extent that patents are not not keeping important drugs from developing countries, but instead are encouraging investment in new and better medicines, America should strongly protest, in any trade negotiations, the intellectual property upon which we build a new medical future. Ultimately, it's Saddam and bin Laden who are America's ene-mies, not the nation's pharmaceutical and biotech firms. How could anyone forget that?"[11]

The idea that any consideration of public interest or ethics is antithetical to the American economy—or even goes against the American way of life—has been used before with property rights: "A blow at slavery is a blow at commerce and civilization," the 1861 Mississippi Secession Declaration reads. That document also spoke of property rights that had to be protected at all costs. "Our position is thoroughly identified with the institution of slavery—the greatest material interest of the world. Its labor supplies the product which constitutes by far the largest and most important portions of commerce of the earth."[12]

Patenting life is not a form of slavery. But the need to keep property laws on the books regardless of ethical considerations has its echoes in slavery and other policies where justice is sacrificed for illusions of economic prosperity.

Goldberg's letter can be countered with an argument that patents on life are, in fact, un-American:

- **Life patents are unconstitutional** because they slow scientific innovation, they do not reward inventors, and they do not serve the public good.

- **Life patents go against a capitalist society** because the monopolies that life patents give on technology and knowledge negate the competitive ideal that pushes private interests to give us ever-better, inexpensive, and widely-available products and technologies.

- **Life patents do not promote the U.S. economy** because, they may be responsible for the demise of the biotech industry. Further, the short-term financial benefits of life patents go to multinational corporations and their investors, not to American companies and the people who support them.

- **Life patents are an abuse of U.S. political and economic power.** Patents on life make our country look like the

colonialist thugs of Europe who raped conquered lands
with their economic and technological might with little
regard for human rights.

- Finally, **life patents are undemocratic** because the policy
has not been decided at the legislative level, or even at the
executive. Awarding patents on life has been arrived at
with no input from voters or their Congressional representatives.

Unheard Voices in an Unheard Debate

In patent applications, the Patent Office converses only
with the applicant. There is no public record of what patents
are currently being considered. No opinions from other scientists, the community or people most affected by the patent, or
by the public at large are considered in the awarding of a patent.
In most cases, these groups find out about the patent only after
it has been awarded. It then takes a costly court battle in order
to fight the patent in any way.

We shouldn't ignore the voice of the biotechnology companies and universities. Admittedly, this book has emphasized
other voices in the debate over and above the industry line. In
this book's defense, however, it is very hard to come up with
demonstrable reasons for the continued existence of life
patents. When pressed, biotechnology spokesmen will drag out
some of the general slogans we have already heard: Life patents
guarantee a return on investments, they create a vibrant
biotechnology industry and U.S. economy, they promote scientific progress, and they are guaranteed by the Constitution.
Rarely, however, are these slogans backed up with data that supports them, or even anecdotes that demonstrate the helpfulness
of life patents in promoting the progress of science and the useful arts. In all my research, I could not find a story of a life
patent that did any of the things that the rhetoric promises, nor
could I find a biotech representative who told of such a story.

The successful companies of the biotech industry—Myriad, Amgen, Human Genome Sciences—are successes of individual companies, not of the entire industry. The successes of those companies, as we have seen, seem to have cost other companies, society, and the progress of science more than they have benefited.

The biotechnology industry and universities maintains their argument, however, that genes and genomes, plants and animals as commodities that can be bought and sold, or monopolized until a product has been developed from them. "Genes are basically chemicals," is their mantra, and should be treated as such.

What are some of the other values given to biological material that the Patent Office does not allow?

For the families of children with Canavan disease who donated tissue and blood in order to increase knowledge of the disease, the value of the biological material is altogether different from that of the hospital that patented it. We are reminded once again of the statement made by the father of two of those children: "What the hospital has done is a desecration of the good that has come from our children's short lives." To desecrate is to take away the sacred character of something. For those families, the biological material of their children held some value beyond their chemical composition. How that biological material would ultimately be used—in this case to boost a hospital's budget—was of concern to the families because the biological material, and the information it held, was a reflection, perhaps a memorial, of their children's short lives.

For Bolivian farmers, quinoa is more than just a set of chemicals. It is even more than just sustenance. It is the food that their fathers grew and their grandfathers and their fathers before them. It is their heritage, an artifact that is a part of their cultural identity. The value that they attribute to quinoa goes beyond monetary worth; the value includes the lifestyle of past generations that will be passed to future generations. The genetic make-up of quinoa—the chemicals of quinoa—are a part of home for Bolivian farmers.

In another instance of differing value, some Icelanders believe that their genetic make-up is a national resource, like the fish that supports their economy. If, as the Iceland Health Sector Database proposes, this national resource is to be bought and sold, then Iceland should get just compensation for it, as any country that sold their national resources would expect to. While the value of their biological material may be ultimately financial, these Icelanders view their genetic make-up as a shared common property. Therefore, any profits garnered by way of their genetic make-up should not go to a single private company, but instead should be shared by Icelandic society at large.

For others in Iceland, and many that critique genetic testing in general, an individual's genetic make-up is extremely personal and should not be sold or shared at all. Individuals who have traditionally been marginalized by society—the ill, physically "impaired," those with mental disorders, and minority and ethnic groups—may be especially suspicious of so-called scientific determinations of their molecular biology. For these groups, the collection and analysis of genetic material appears to be yet another way of setting up social categories and institutionalizing prejudice. The value that they attribute to their biological data is associated with the power that such knowledge, faulty or not, will bring to those who control and are able to manipulate it, whether it be a government, insurance companies, or society at large.

Even within the research community, any one DNA segment, genetically manipulated plant or mammal, will have a multitude of values, above and beyond that which is attributed by the patent office. The CCR5 was merely another genetic tract among hundreds that Human Genome Sciences claimed in a patent. For other scientists who worked for years on the AIDS virus, the CCR5 was much more important to their research. The now-numerous "breast cancer" genes have a financial importance to a biotechnology company because the company can make money from genetic tests. Other researchers may give a different value to BRCA genes because they believe studying that particular biological material may help in discovering some of the actual causes of breast cancer instead of just a quick product of questionable veracity.

There is yet another value attributed to our biology for many scientists who do not parrot the biotechnology industry's rhetoric of genes being merely chemicals. It is value that comes from the awe of working with a complex, dynamic, nearly incomprehensible system that is life. Upon receiving his Nobel Prize, Donald J. Cram said, "Few scientists acquainted with the chemistry of biological systems at the molecular level can avoid being inspired. Evolution has produced chemical compounds that are exquisitely organized to accomplish the most complicated and delicate of tasks."[13]

With all these voices and with all the values attributed to genes, genomes, plants and animals, how are we to form national policy on life patents?

Arriving at Policy the Old Fashioned Way: Democratically

It is true that it will be impossible to please all these voices, and to create national policy that respects all the values given to genes and objects of life patents. As exemplified by the stem cell debate, there will always be a segment of the population who will be disappointed and disagree with any policy. That is the nature of democracy.

But the important thing is that a debate, some kind of a discussion, about life patents occurs so that the country can consciously decide—democratically decide—on the issue of life patents.

Even if a final policy does not reflect the many values described in this book, the voices describing these values must be heard. Democracy requires these voices be heard for such an important decision as allowing patents on life. Our country guarantees that they should be heard with unalienable rights such as freedom of speech.

Although recent discussions regarding free speech involve the media or individuals whose art forms conflict with certain cultural norms, a glance at the legal history of the right to free speech illuminates another aspect: the right for society to have access to a multitude of ideas and to hear from differing value systems. In order to arrive at a democratic value which will drive governmental policy, all values in a society must be weighed and heard from. This idea—that a democratic society profits from hearing many different ideas and differing sets of values and thereby arrives at just democratic policies—derived its reasoning from science itself. Oliver Wendell Holmes first took the scientific method and applied it to justice and democracy as a whole with his theory of a "marketplace of ideas."

> If you have no doubt of your premises or your power and want a certain result with all your heart you naturally express your wishes in law and sweep away all opposition... But when men have realized that time has upset many fighting faiths, they may come to believe even more than they believe the very foundations of their own conduct that the ultimate good desired is better reached by free trade in ideas—that the best test of truth is the power of that thought to get itself accepted in the competition of the market, and that truth is the only ground upon which their wishes safely can be carried out. That at any rate is the theory of our Constitution. It is an experiment, as all life is an experiment.[14]

Ideas and values for a democratic society are like ideas in science: They must be tested against other values before they can be considered just and democratic. It is not that policy will be arrived at which will please all parties, or that a compromise will be achieved in which all voices and values are equally respected. Rather, policy will be established after these voices have bounced off of each other, been compared, tested and analyzed in the "free market of ideas." In a democracy, it is not necessary that policy be directly decided by these voices, merely that these voices be heard.

Awarding patents on life works against a truly democratic discussion about what value molecular biological material should be given by policy. As it stands now, patent policy restricts that debate to discussions between the Patent Office and the lawyers of universities and corporations and how they value their "inventions." This is a valorization which the universities and companies see as just, but it is not a democratic valorization.

It has been suggested that a more democratic forum than the Patent Office could be created in the form of a regulatory body—similar to the Food and Drug Administration (FDA) or Federal Aviation Agency (FAA)—that would control and create policy on such biological "inventions," judging each within their specific context. The FAA is an especially apt model as it was developed from a need to balance patent protection with the dissemination of upstream knowledge in order for aerospace technology to progress.

Some, like author Seth Shulman, suggest a "zoning commission" for this uncharted area. This zoning commission would consider the complicated policy issues that the biotechnology industry currently faces and will continue to face: "[We] need a public policy body tasked with balancing and nurturing the partnership between the private and public sectors that have brought us to this stage in our understanding of the human genome."[15]

Regardless of the form such a body ultimately takes, it is important that it be guided by the right to free speech in which the ultimate value given such inventions are reached in as democratic a manner as possible. If exclusive property rights are deemed appropriate to certain of these biological "inventions," then the regulatory body must further be guided by the Constitutional mandate that these rights both promote science and give due credit to the actual "inventor(s)" of the invention. What is of paramount importance is that such a regulatory body be continually open to public comment, not just from scientists, universities, and private companies, but from all citizens whose values must be considered in order to arrive at a policy.

Even before such a commission is considered, however, Congress may need to take the Supreme Court's hint and make a conscious decision to accept, limit, or reject patents on life. Past attempts have been minimal or ignored. Many of the quotes in this book have been taken from defendants of life patents who stood before a single Congressional subcommittee in 2000. That subcommittee, on Courts and Intellectual Property Rights, took biotech's side and decided, once again, to not decide.

In February 2002, Representatives Lynn Rivers (D-MI) and David Weldon (R-FL) introduced two bills concerning life patents. The first bill "exempts from patent infringement those individuals who use patented genetic sequence information for noncommercial research purposes."[16] The bill basically allows researchers who use genetic tests for purely research or diagnostic purposes the ability to do so without fear of patent infringement. The second bill would mandate an in depth study of gene patents and their affect on industry and scientific progress.

"Current patenting policies do not serve the broader interests of patients," Representative Lynn Rivers explained when she introduced the bills. "Enactment of H.R. 3967 would ensure that the fantastic advances in medical genetics are fully harnessed not just for the benefit of patent holders, but also for the broader public."[17]

Both bills have been referred to the House Subcommittee on Courts, the Internet, and Intellectual Property. Lynn Rivers was not reelected to the House in 2003. What may have been the beginning of a national discussion on life patents seems to have been placed in the black hole of Congress known as "in committee."

But the harm caused by life patents will not go away. At this moment, monopolies are being placed on genes, plants and animals, and even whole human beings. Patents on life continue to be given under the nose of the public and to the detriment of science, society and individual patients. The biotech industry is destroying itself through monopolies on upstream knowledge and litigation costs. In a few decades, we may view life patents as not only the biggest swindle, but also the biggest economic and scientific mistake we have made in the 21st century. Like the patent system of the 18th century British crown or the era of European colonialism, will we see the policy of awarding life patents collapse under its own injustices?

Let us hope not. The real promises of genetic research depend upon a conscious decision.

Epilogue

As we learn more and more about our molecular biology, we're discovering that the majority of it is controlled by patents. As this book goes to press, scientists are making strides in discovering a myriad of functions for the so-called "junk DNA"—the 95% of our DNA that does not appear to code proteins. Scientists, however, are not free to explore junk DNA. They must pay licensing fees to a company called Genetic Technologies that patented junk DNA and all of its functions in every species on earth in the mid 1990s. In other words, one company owns 95% of the DNA in humans, plants, and animals. The patent was awarded before anyone had really found a specific function for the DNA. Ironically, the scientist who filed the patent, Dr. Malcolm Stones, receives no part of the millions of dollars, perhaps billions, that Genetic Technologies could now earns from licensing the patent. Stones resigned from Genetic Technologies' in 2000 before the money started rolling in. In the meantime, once again, licensing fees, law suits, and the walls of patent protection keep scientists from doing their jobs: exploring our biology and discovering its secrets.

Notes

INTRODUCTION

1 Peter Gorner, "Parents Suing over Patenting of Genetic Test," *The Chicago Tribune*, November 19, 2000.

2 Arthur Allen, "Who owns your DNA?" Salon.com, March 7, 2000, retrieved from www.salon.com/health/feature/2000/03/07/genetic_tests-/index.html, October 23, 2001.

3 Gorner. See also Eliot Marshall, "Families Sue Hospital, Scientist for Control of Canavan Gene," *Science* 290, (November 10, 2000): 1062.

4 K. Rafinski, "Hospital's Patent Stokes Debate on Human Genes," *Miami Herald*, November 14, 1999 cited in Jon F. Merz, "Discoveries: Are There Limits on What May be Patented?" in *Who Owns Life?* (Amherst, New York: Prometheus Press, 2002).

5 The numbers of life patents waiting and already awarded by the U.S.P.T.O. seem to vary greatly depending on who is asked in the patent office. In an August 2001 issue of *Scientific American*, John J. Doll, director of biotechnology for the U.S.P.T.O. claimed that 20,000 patents on genes or gene-related molecules from all life forms have been patented and that there are 25,000 applications in waiting. One year earlier, the former director of the U.S.P.T.O. told a Congressional subcommittee that there had been only 6,000 patents awarded on the genetic make-up of all life forms and only 1,000 of those were from human genes. 20,000 gene patents were pending, he said. Either the number of life patents being awarded has grown exponentially or the U.S.P.T.O. really has little idea how many life patents they have given out. I suspect the former. "Talking Gene Patents," *Scientific American*, August 2001, 28 and "Gene Patents and Other Genomic Inventions" *Hearing before the Subcommittee on Courts and Intellectual Property of the Committee on the Judiciary House of Representatives*, 106th Congress, Second Session, July 13, 2000, retrieved from www.house.gov/judiciary/scot0713.htm.

6 Kies' patent covered a new process for weaving straw with silk or thread. "Patent Points to Ponder—Mothers of Invention," retrieved from http://inventors.about.com/library/inventors/bblkiprimer6_12w.htm.

7 Vandana Shiva, "North-South Conflicts in Intellectual Property Rights," *Peace Review* 12:4 (2000): 508.

8 Prepared statement of Todd Dickinson, Subcommittee on Courts and Intellectual Property, Committee of the Judiciary, House of Representatives, July 13, 2000, retrieved from www.house.gov/judiciary-/scot0713.htm.

9   The World Trade Organization agreement on Trade-Related Aspects of Intellectual Property Rights (TRIPS) excludes plants and animals from patent laws but, under its auspices, all countries that sign it must allow patents on microorganisms and provide for some sort of patent intellectual property protection for *sui generis* (unique) type of plant varieties. On top of this, much stricter patent protection for plants and animals is being guaranteed through closed bilateral treaties between developed countries and the South. See "'TRIPS-plus' Through the Back Door," by GRAIN in cooperation with the South Asian Network for Food, Ecology and Culture (SANFEC), July 2001 retrieved from GRAIN's website at http://www.grain.org.

10 Alice Domurat Dreger, "Metaphors of Morality," *Controlling Our Destinies: Historical, Philosophical, Ethical, and Theological Perspectives on the Human Genome Project*, ed. Phillip R. Sloan, (Notre Dame, Indiana: University of Notre Dame Press, 2000), 166.

11 Paula Kiberstis and Leslie Roberts, "It's Not Just in the Genes," *Science* 296, (April 26, 2002): 693.

12 Walter C. Willett, "Balancing Life-Style and Genomics Research for Disease Prevention," *Science* 296, (April 26, 2002): 695—698.

13 Willett, 21.

14 Executive Summary, Incyte Genomics Inc. Testimony of Randal Scott, Subcommittee on Courts and Intellectual Property, Committee of the Judiciary, House of Representatives, July 13, 2000, retrieved from www.house.gov/judiciary/scot0713.htm.

15 Ellen Goodman, "Swept Away in a Gold Rush to Cash in on Our Genes," *Boston Globe*, March 5, 2000.

16 Jenna Greene, "He's Not Just Monkeying Around," *Legal Times*, August 16, 1999.

17 From statements given to the United States House of Representatives Subcommittee on Courts and intellectual Property by Todd Dickinson, Director of the U.S.P.T.O. Oversight Hearing on Gene Patents and Other Genomic Inventions, July 13, 2000, 32-33.

CHAPTER ONE

1   Blumenthal uses the Einstein quote in the introduction to his study. David Blumenthal, "Withholding Research Results in Academic Life Science: Evidence From a National Survey of Faculty," *Journal of the American Medical Association* 277, (April 16, 1997).

2   Kevin Davies, *Cracking the Genome* (New York, New York: The Free Press, 2001), 83.

3   "Patenting Breast Cancer," retrieved from University of New South Wales Council for Civil Liberties web page at www.nswccl.org.au.

4   Davies, 83.

5   Davies, 83.

6   Deborah Smith, "Who Owns Your DNA?" *Sidney Morning Herald*, March 14, 2001. Bruce was part of a consortium of European churches that opposed the BRCA1 patent. The SRT Project is an arm of the Church of Scotland and can be found at http://dspace.dial.pipex.com/srtscot/srt-page3.shtml

7   "Myriad Genetics Awarded BRCA1 Composition of Matter Patent," Press Release, Myriad Genetics Inc., May 5, 1998, retrieved from Myriad web page at www.myriad.com.

8   "Partners and Collaborators," retrieved from the Myriad web page: www.myriad.com,

9   *Myriad Genetics 1998 Annual Report*, Letter to Shareholders, 3.

10 David K. Stone and Eric T. Schmidt, "Myriad Genetics," *Biotechnology Quarterly*, July 1998.

11 Steve Bunk, "Researchers Feel Threatened by Disease Gene Patents," *The Scientist* 13, #20, (October 11, 1999): 7.

12 Julian Borger, "Gene Patents Hit Research," *The Guardian*, December 15, 1999.

13 Steve Bunk, "Researchers Feel Threatened by Disease Gene Patents," *The Scientist* 13, #20, (October 11, 1999): 7.

14 Meredith Wadman, "Testing Time for Gene Patent as Europe Rebels," *Nature* 413 (October 4, 2001): 443.

15 Wadman, 443.

16 Scientists, law experts, and the public at large have criticized the increasing secret nature of scientific research in the quest for proprietary rights. Among some notable articles:

    • Jonathon King and Doreen Stabinsky, "Patents on Cells, Genes, and Organisms Undermine the Exchange of Scientific Ideas," *The Chronicle of Higher Education*, February 5, 1999.

    • Jon F. Merz, Mildred K. Cho, Madeline J. Robertson, and Debra G.B. Leonard, "Disease Gene Patenting is a Bad Innovation," *Molecular Diagnosis* 2, No. 4, (December 1997).

17 Eliot Marshall, "Is Data-Hoarding Slowing the Assault on Pathogens?" *Science* 275, (February 7, 1997): 777.

18 "House of Lords Select Committee on Science and Technology," Seventh Report, Appendix 6:101, March 17, 1998.

19 Lewis Thomas, *The Youngest Science: Notes of a Medicine-Watcher*, (New York, New York: Bantam Books, 1983), 35.

20 "Revised Final FY 1999 Performance Plan and FY 2000 Performance Plan: IV," retrieved from the Council for Disease Control at www.cdc.gov.

21 "House of Lords Select Committee," Appendix 6:8.

22 Retrieved from NIAID Website: www.niaid.nih.gov/, October, 2001.

23 Hazel Muir, "Bug Uncovered", New Scientist.com April 20, 2001. www.newscientist.com

24 "Gene Patents and Other Genomic Inventions" *Hearing before the Subcommittee on Courts and Intellectual Property of the Committee on the Judiciary House of Representatives*, 106th Congress, Second Session, July 13, 2000, 56.

25 Marlene Cimons and Paul Jacobs, "Biotech Battlefield: Profits vs. Public," *LA Times*, February 21, 1999.

26 Marshall, "Data Hoarding," 778.

27 In September 2001, the Staphlab at the university announced that they had completed the sequencing for a particular staph genome. The data is directly available and free over the internet. Retrieved from University of Oklahoma web site: www.genome.ou.edu/staph.html, October 2001.

28 Marshall, "Data Hoarding," 777.

29 Cimmons and Jacobs, "Battlefield."

30 Cimmons and Jacobs, "Battlefield."

31 Cimmons and Jacobs, "Battlefield."

32 Cimmons and Jacobs, "Battlefield."

33 O. Cosivi, J.M Grange, C.J. Daborn, M.C. Raviglione, et.al. "Zoonotic Tuberculosis due to Mycobacterium bovis in Developing Countries," *Emerging Infectious Diseases* 4., No. 1,(January – March 1998).

34 *Tuberculosis Fact Sheet #104*, World Health Organization, Revised August 2002, retrieved from www.who.int/mediacentre/factsheets/who104/en/

35 *Ending Neglect*, ed. Lawrence Geiter, Committee on the Elimination of Tuberculosis in the United States, Institute of Medicine (Washington, D.C: National Academy Press, 2000), 136-137.

36 Marshall, "Data Hoarding," 778.

37 Marshall, "Data Hoarding," 777.

38 Marshall, "Data Hoarding," 777–780.

39 Antonio Regalado, "Scientists' Hunt for SARS Cure Turns to Race for Patent Rights," *Wall Street Journal*, May 5, 2003.

40 Kevin Conner, "Cash Grab on Virus Patents: Doctors Worry Trend Will Interfere with Finding SARS Vaccine," *Toronto Sun*, May 7, 2003.

41 George Weinstock, "Genomics and Bacterial Pathogenesis," *Emerging Infectious Diseases* 6, No. 5, (September – October 2000): 498.

42 Weinstock, 502.

43 David Blumenthal, "Withholding Research Results in Academic Life Science: Evidence From a National Survey of Faculty," *Journal of the American Medical Association* 277, (April 16, 1997).

44 Eric G. Campbell, Brian Clarridge, Manjusha Gokhale, Lauren Bbirenbaum, Stephen Higartner, Neil Holtzman, David Blumenthal, "Data Withholding in Academic Genetics," *Journal of the American Medical Association*, Vol. 287 No. 4, January 23/30, 2002.

45 Jennifer C. Christiansen, "The Price of Silence," *Scientific American*, November 1996.

46 Blumenthal, (1997).

47 Steven A. Rosenberg, "Secrecy in Medical Research," *The New England Journal of Medicine* 334, no. 6 (February 8, 1996): 392-394,

48 Christiansen, "Price."

49 Paul Jacobs and Peter G. Gosselin, "Errors Found in Patent for AIDS Gene, Scientists Say," *Los Angeles Times*, March 21, 2000.

50 Eliot Marshall, "Patent on HIV Receptor Provokes an Outcry," *Science* 287, (February 25, 2000): 1375.

51 "HIV/AIDS/STI Surveillance," retrieved from," *Communicable Disease Surveillance and Response (CSR) Web Page*, at www.who.int/emc/diseases, October, 2000.

52 Paul Jacobs and Peter G. Gosselin, "'Robber Barons of the Genetic Age': Experts Fret Over Effect of Gene Patents on Research," *Los Angeles Times*, February 28, 2000.

53 "Bloomberg.com Financial Market Commodities News," retrieved from Company Graphs, www.bloomberg.com, October 26, 2000.

54 Marshal, "Patent on HIV," 1377.

55 Paul Jacobs and Peter G. Gosselin, "'Robber Barons of the Genetic Age': Experts Fret Over Effect of Gene Patents on Research," *Los Angeles Times*, February 28, 2000.

56 Burke, et. al. "Letter to Commissioner of Patents and Trademarks," Comment 42, National Advisory Council for Human Genome Research, National Institutes of Health, March 21, 2000.

57 Jacobs and Gosselin, "Robber Barons."

58 Paul Jacobs and Peter G. Gosselin, "Errors Found in Patent for AIDS Gene, Scientists Say," *Los Angeles Times*, March 21, 2000

59 Marshal, "Patent on HIV," 1377.

60 Jacobs and Gosselin, "Errors."

61 Burke, et. al. "Letter to Commissioner of Patents and Trademarks," Comment 42, National Advisory Council for Human Genome Research, National Institutes of Health, March 21, 2000.

62 David Malakoff, "Will a Smaller Genome Complicated the Patent Chase?" *Science*, Vol. 291, February 16, 2001, 1194.

63 Malakoff, "Smaller Genome."

64 Jacobs and Gosselin, "Robber Barons."

65 Jacobs and Gosselin, "Robber Barons."

66 Jon F. Merz, "Disease Gene Patents: Overcoming Unethical Constraints on Clinical Laboratory Medicine," *Clinical Chemistry* 45, (1999) :324-330.

67 Anna Schissel, Jon F. Merz, and Mildred K. Cho, "Survey Confirms Fears About Licensing of Genetic Tests," *Nature* 402, (11 November 11, 1999): 118.

68 Vida Foubister, "Gene Patents Raise Concerns for Researchers, Clinicians," *American Medical News*, February 21, 2000.

69 John Barton, "Reforming the Patent System," *Science* 287, (March 17, 2000): 1933. Originally taken from a survey by the American Intellectual Property Law Association (AIPLA), "Report of Economic Survey 1999," (AIPLA, Arlington, VA, 1999), tables 21 and 22.

70 Fred Warshofsky, *The Patent Wars: The Battle to Own the World's Technology* (New York, New York: John Wiley & Sons, 1994), 247.

71 Julian Borger, "Gene Patents Hit Research," *The Guardian*, December 15, 1999.

72 Vida Foubister, "Gene Patents Raise Concerns for Researchers, Clinicians," *American Medical News*, February 21, 2000.

73 "American College of Medical Genetics position statement on gene patents and accessibility of gene testing," *Genetics in Medicine* I, no. 5, 237.

74 "Patenting the Human Genome," American Medical Association web page retrieved from their policy finder at http://ama-assn.org/apps/, November 13, 2001.

75 Jennifer C. Christiansen, "The Price of Silence," *Scientific American*, November 1996.

76 "Largest Increase in History for Federal R & D," *Science and Technology in Congress*, American Association for the Advancement of Science, January 2002.

77 Marlene Cimons and Paul Jacobs, "Biotech Battlefield: Profits vs. Public," *LA Times*, February 21, 1999.

78 "Human Genome Project Information," retrieved from U.S.D.O.E. web site, www.ornl.gov/hgmis, January 30, 2001.

79 "Human Genome Project Information," retrieved from U.S.D.O.E. web site, www.ornl.gov/hgmis, on January 30, 2001.

80 *Ending Neglect*, ed. Lawrence Geiter, Committee on the Elimination of Tuberculosis in the United States, Institute of Medicine (Washington, D.C: National Academy Press, 2000), 140.

81 Lita Nelsen, "The Rise of Intellectual Property Protection in the American University," *Science* 279, (March 6, 1998).

82 "Oversight Hearing on Gene Patents and Other Genomic Inventions," July 13, 2000, page 129.

83 Gretchen Vogel, "A Scientific Result without the Science," *Science*, Vol. 276, May 30, 1997.

84 Fred Warshofsky, *The Patent Wars: The Battle to Own the World's Technology* (New York, New York: John Wiley & Sons, 1994), 30.

85 Tom Abate, "Do Gene Patents Wrap Research in Red Tape?" *The San Francisco Chronicle*, March 25, 2002.

86 Matt Fleischer, "Patent Thyself," *The American Lawyer*, June 21, 2001.

87 Fleischer, "Patent Thyself."

88 James Meek, "Poet Attempts the Ultimate in Self-Invention – Patenting her Own Genes," *Guardian*, February 29, 2000.

CHAPTER TWO

1 Madeleine Bunting, "The Profits that Kill: Intellectual Property Agreements are making too much money for the west," *The Guardian*, February 12, 2001.

2 Stephanie Howard, *Life, Lineage and Sustenance: Indigenous Peoples and Genetic Engineering: Threats to Food, Agriculture, and the Environment*, (Indigenous Peoples Council on Biocolonialism, September 2001), 14.

3 Vandana Shiva, "North-South Conflicts in Intellectual Property Rights," *Peace Review* 12:4 (2000): 508.

4 Colin Woodard, "U.S. Patents on Living Things Irk Some," *Christian Science Monitor*, August 1, 1999.

5 "No Patents on Rice! No Patents on Life! Statement from peoples' movements and NGOs across Asia," retrieved from Genetic Resources Action International (GRAIN) website, http://www.grain.org/publications/rice-no-patents-en.cfm.

6 Shiva, "North-South Conflicts," 501-508.

7 Andrew Pollack, "The Green Revolution Yields to the Bottom Line," *The New York Times*, May 15, 2001.

8 *J.E.M. Ag Supply Inc. v. Pioneer Hi-Bred International Inc.*, No. 99-1996.

9   Linda Greenhouse, "Supreme Court Roundup," *The New York Times*, December 11, 2001.

10 "1996 Biopiracy Update: Bolivian Quinoa Claimed in U.S. Patent," ETC Group Communiqué, December 30, 1996, retrieved from www.rafi.org., January 28, 2002.

11 "Quinoa Patent Dropped: Andean Farmers Defeat U.S. University," ETC Group Genotype, May 22, 1998, retrieved from www.rafi.org.

12 "Quinoa Patent Dropped," ETC.

13 *The ETC Century*, Rural Advancement Foundation International (RAFI) Occasional Paper Series: OP61, October 5, 1999, 40.

14 Paul W. Heisey, C.S. Srinivasan, and Colin Thirtle, "Public Sector Plant Breeding in a Privatizing World," Economic Research Service, USDA, Agriculture Information Bulletin No. 772, August 2001, 1.

15 Andrew Pollack, "The Green Revolution Yields to the Bottom Line," *The New York Times*, May 15, 2001.

16 Heisey, et.al., iii.

17 Heisey, et.al., iii.

18 Seth Shulman, *Owning the Future*, (New York: Houghton Mifflin Company, 1999), 90.

19 Shulman, *Owning the Future*, 103. In the end, the farmers refused to sign the contract and the stipulation was removed.

20 "Sask Farmer Wins Hearing from Supreme Court in Patent Battle with Monsanto," *Canadian Press*, May 8, 2003.

21 Martin Teitel and Kimberly A. Wilson, *Genetically Engineered Food: Changing the Nature of Nature*, (Rochester, Vermont: Park Street Press, 2001), 98-99.

22 Winona LaDuke, "Wild Rice Meeting to Stop the Bio-Pirates," May 2002, *DeBahJiMon Online*, retrieved from www.leechlakeojibwe.org/debahji-mon/archives/s00sissues/may2002/wildrice.shtml

23 Winona LaDuke, "Wild Rice: Maps, Genes, & Patents," *The Circle: Native American News and Arts* 22, Issue 10, (October 2001).

24 Lewontin, R.C. "People are not Commodities," *New York Times*, August 2, 1999.

25 Kari Stefansson, "The Icelandic Healthcare Database: A Tool to Create Knowledge, A Social Debate, and a Bioethical and Privacy Challenge," *Who Owns Our Genes?* Proceedings of an International Conference, October 1999, Tallinn, Estonia, Organised by the Nordic Committee on Bioethics, 24.

26 "DeCode Files Patents on 350 Drug Targets – All with Population Linkage Data in Major Diseases," Press Release, November 7, 2001, retrieved from deCode website at www.decode.com/news

27 Tomas Soega and Bogi Andersen, "The Icelandic Health Sector Database: deCode and the "New" Ethics for Genetic Research," *Who Owns Our Genes?* Proceedings of an International Conference, October 1999, Tallinn, Estonia, Organised by the Nordic Committee on Bioethics, 42.

28 Kaiser, 1160.

29 Pomfret and Nelson wrote a series of five investigative articles on medical trials conducted in developing countries. John Pomfret and Deborah Nelson, "The Body Hunters, Part 4: In Rural China, A Genetic Mother Lode," *The Washington Post*, Wednesday, December 20, 2000.

30 Hilary Rose, "The Commodification of Bioinformation: The Icelandic Health Sector Database," (London, England: The Wellcome Trust, 2001), 26-29.

31 Ross Anderson, *The deCode Proposal for an Icelandic Health Database*, October 20, 1998, 11.

32 Stefansson, 23.

33 Pomfret and Nelson, "The Body Hunters, Part 4."

34 Rose, 17.

35 Iceland is considered the second most expensive country to live in, after Japan. See Graeme Cornwallis and Deanna Swaney, *Iceland, Greenland & the Faroe Islands*, (Melbourne, Australia: Lonely Planet Publications, 2001).

36 Kita MacPherson, Tapping Iceland's Genetic Jackpot," *The Star-Ledger* (New Jersey), December 17, 2000.

37 Jocelyn Kaiser, "Private Biobanks Spark Ethical Concerns," *Science* 298, (November 8, 2002): 1160.

38 Tomas Soega and Bogi Andersen, "The Icelandic Health Sector Database: deCode and the "New" Ethics for Genetic Research," *Who Owns Our Genes?* Proceedings of an International Conference, October 1999, Tallinn, Estonia, Organised by the Nordic Committee on Bioethics, 40, 41.

39 Einar Arnason and Frank Wells, "Icelandic Heterogeneity and false positives," *Sunday Telegraph*, September 10, 2000.

40 Andrew Pollack, "Large DNA File to Help Track Illness in Blacks," *New York Times*, May 27, 2003.

41 Paula Kiberstis and Leslie Roberts, "It's Not Just the Genes," *Science* 296, (April 26, 2002). Kiberstis and Roberts draw this conclusion from a study on Schizophrenia in the same volume: Douglas F. Levinson, et.al. "No

Major Schizophrenia Locus Detected on Chromosome 1q in a Large Multicenter Sample," 739.

42 Jocelyn Kaiser, "Population Databases Boom, From Iceland to the U.S.," *Science* 298, (November 8, 2002).

43 Henry T. Greely and Mary-Claire King, "Letter to Government of Iceland," retrieved from http://www.mannvernd.is/english/articles /greely_king&_ing-e.html.

44 Soega and Andersen, 53.

45 Edmund J. Pratt, "Intellectual Property," retrieved from Pfizer Inc. web page at www.pfizer.com/are/about_public-/mn_about_intellectual-propfrm.htMl.

46 *Integrating Intellectual Property Rights and Developmental Policy: Report of the Commission on Intellectual Property Rights*, (London, England: Commission on Intellectual Property Rights, September 2002), retrieved from www.iprcommission.org

47 "Patently Problematic," *The Economist*, September 14, 2002, 75.

48 "Patenting, Piracy, and Perverted Promises: Patents on Life: The Last Assault on the Commons," Genetic Resources Action International (GRAIN) retrieved from www.grain.org/publications/piracy-en-p.htm.

49 "About Lilly: Overview: Position on Key Issues," retrieved from Eli Lilly web page at http://www.lilly.com

50 Stephanie Nolen, "Stephen Lewis Has One Word For Us: Help," *The Globe And Mail*, January 4, 2003.

51 "Stark Warning over Aids Apathy," BBC News, July 10, 2000, retrieved from http://news.bbc.co.uk on March 8, 2001.

52 Arthur Miller & Michael Davis, *Intellectual Property: Patents, Trademarks, and Copyright In A Nutshell*, (St. Paul, Minnesota: West Group, 2000), 438.

53 Simon Taylor, "Drug Firms Fight Lamy 'Threat' to Patents on Life-saving Medicines," *European Voice*, March 9-15, 2000.

54 Taylor, "Drug Firms Fight Lamy."

55 British Parliament member Glenys Kinnock coined the phrase. "South Africa Fights Over AIDS Drugs," (Associated Press), *The New York Times*, March 5, 2001.

56 "South Africa Fights Over Aids Drugs," (AP) *The New York Times*, March 5, 2001.

57 Stephen Lewis, "J'Accuse: The West is Willfully Turning Its Back on the Greatest Human Tragedy of our Age," Speaker's Corner, National Speakers Bureau, January 26, 2001, retrieved from http://www.nsb.com/cornerfebmar01.asp

58 Stephen Lewis, "J'Accuse: The West is Willfully Turning Its Back on the Greatest Human Tragedy of our Age," Speaker's Corner, National Speakers Bureau, January 26, 2001, retrieved from http://www.nsb.com/cornerfebmar01.asp

59 William Greider, *One World, Ready of Not*, (New York, New York: Simon and Schuster, 1997), 139.

60 Aileen Kwa, "WTO and Developing Countries," *Foreign Policy – Infocus* 3, no. 37, (November 1998).

61 "HHS, Bayer Agree to Cipro Purchase," U.S. Department of Health & Human Services Press Release, October 24, 2001.

62 John le Carre, "In Place of Nations," *The Nation*, April 9, 2001.

CHAPTER THREE

1 Barry Commoner, "Unraveling the DNA Myth: The Spurious Foundation of Genetic Engineering," *Harper's Magazine*, February, 2002.

2 "Dolly was a Red Herring," *The Economist*, May 1, 2003.

3 Advertisement for Agilent Technologies, *New York Times*, September 1, 1999, B10.

4 William Schwartz, *Life Without Disease*, (Berkeley, California: University of California Press, 1998), 1.

5 Alice Domurat Dreger, "Metaphors of Morality," *Controlling Our Destinies: Historical, Philosophical, Ethical, and Theological Perspectives on the Human Genome Project*, ed. Phillip R. Sloan, (Notre Dame, Indiana: University of Notre Dame Press, 2000), 166.

6 Sheldon Rampton and John Stauber, *Trust Us We're Experts*, (New York, New York: Jeremy P. Tarcher/Putnam, 2001), 201.

7 Rampton and Stauber, *Toxic Sludge is Good for You! Lies, Damn Lies, and the Public Relations Industry*, (Monroe, Maine: Common Courage Press, 1995), 34.

8 "Nuclear Energy: No solution to Climate Change, A background paper," retrieved from http://archive.greenpeace.org/~comms/no.nukes/-nen-stcc.html#1

9 "Cancelled US commercial Nuclear Power Reactors" and "Permanently Shutdown Nuclear Power Plants," Nuclear Energy Institute, retrieved from http://www.nei.org

10 "Guideline for Environmental Assessment of Energy and Industry Projects," World Bank technical paper No. 154/1992, Environmental Assessment Sourcebook, Vol. III quoted in "Nuclear Energy: No solution to Climate Change, A background paper," retrieved from http://archive.greenpeace.org/~comms/no.nukes/nenstcc.html#1

11 Chris Baltimore, "Texas Reactor Leak Rattles U.S. Nuclear Industry," Reuters, May 1, 2003.

12 Richard Preston, "The Genome Warrior," *The New Yorker* 19, (2000): 68.

13 "U.S. Nuclear Power Plants: General Statistics," Nuclear Energy Institute, retrieved from http://www.nei.org/doc.asp?catnum=3&catid=13&docid=&format=print

14 Some would disagree with the idea that "biotechnology is based on real science." Biologist, educator, and activist Barry Commoner continues to insist that many of scientists' basic beliefs on DNA are demonstrably wrong, specifically the idea that DNA is self-replicating. "It is a truism that in our society, such a new industry is created not for the purpose of enhancing scientific understanding, but in the hope of a competitive financial return. Unfortunately, the science on which biotechnology is founded has become, to a large extent, distorted by this process as well, and is itself in need of critical revision." Barry Commoner, "Unraveling the Secret of Life: DNA self-duplication, the basic precept of biotechnology, is denied," *GeneWatch*, Vol. 16, Num. 3, May-June 2003. See also Barry Commoner, "Unraveling the DNA Myth: The Spurious Foundation of Genetic Engineering," *Harper's Magazine*, February, 2002. Commoner may yet prove all of biotechnology, and this writer, wrong.

15 Sara Chandros Hull and Kiran Prasad, "Direct-to-Consumer Advertising of Genetic Testing," *Hastings Center Report*, May-June 2001, 33.

16 Jing-Shiarn Wang, Ronald R. Knipling, and Lawrence J. Blincoe, "The Dimensions of Motor Vehicle Crash Risk," *Journal of Transportation and Statistics* 2, no. 1, (May 1999): 26.

17 The 1 in 8 statistic, published by the American Cancer Society, does not mean that, in a room with eight randomly selected women, one of them will develop breast cancer. A number of genetic and environmental factors affect women of different ages, increasing or decreasing their chances of cancer throughout their life span depending on these factors. Even at age seventy, only one in 25 women will develop breast cancer over the next ten years. The best way to describe the statistics would be to have a room with one eighty-year-old woman. There is a 1 in 8 chance that she either has already had breast cancer or that she will have breast cancer before she dies. Retrieved from *American Cancer Society Web Page*, National Breast Cancer Awareness Month, October 10, 2000, www.cancer.org.

18 "Genetic Testing for Hereditary Breast and Ovarian Cancer," retrieved from Myriad Web Page, www.myriad.com, September, 2000.

19 "The Role of Genetic Susceptibility Testing for Breast & Ovarian Cancer," ed. Patti Fitzgerald, AMA, a pamphlet published by the

American Medical Association, April, 1999. Two of the writers of the pamphlet were members of the Clinical Advisory Board of Myriad Genetics but "neither Dr. Davis or Ms. Calzone had anything to disclose."

20 Colin B. Begg, "On the Use of Familial Aggregation in Population-Based Case Probands for Calculating Penetrance," *Journal of the National Cancer Institute* 94, no. 16, (August 21, 2002): 1221-1226.

21 Paul Recer, "Studies May Distort Gene Cancer Tie," *Associated Press*, August 21, 2002.

22 Recer

23 Fitzgerald, "Role," 8.

24 Retrieved from *American Cancer Society Web Page*, National Breast Cancer Awareness Month, October 12, 2000, www.cancer.org.

25 From a Swiss-Re pamphlet entitled "Genetic Engineering and Insurance. The Weight of Public Opinion," quoted in Benoit and Kalan, "Genetic Tests and Health Insurance: A Future Divided," *le Monde Diplomatique*, May 2000.

26 Fitzgerald, "Role," 2.

27 Wylie Burke and Melissa A. Austin, "Genetic Risk in Context: Calculating the Penetrance of BRCA1 and BRCA2 Mutations," *Journal of the National Cancer Institute*, Vol. 94, No. 16, 1185-1187, August 21, 2002.

28 "Gene Patents Detrimental to Care, Training, Research," College of American Pathologists Position Paper, retrieved from http://www.cap.orgg/html/advocacy/issues/genetalk.html.

29 Eliot Marshall, "Gene Tests Get Tested," *Science* 275, (February 7, 1997): 782.

30 "Genetic Testing for Breast Cancer Risk: It's Your Choice," retrieved from CancerNet: A Service of the National Cancer Institute, at www.cancer-net.nci.nih.gov/, August 7, 2000.

31 Sharon Begley, "Screening for Genes: Matching Medications to Your Genetic Heritage," *Newsweek*, February 8, 1999.

32 Enrico Bastianelli, Jurg Eckhardt, and Olivier Teirlynck, "Pharma: Can the Middle Hold?" *The McKinsey Quarterly*, 2001, Number 1.

33 "Position Statement on Gene Patents and Accessibility of Gene Testing," American College of Medical Genetics, retrieved from http://www.faseb.org/genetics/acmg/pol-34.htm

34 *Prenatal Testing and Disability Rights*, ed. Erik Parens and Adrienne Asch (Washington, D.C.: Georgetown University Press, 2000), 3.

35 Recer

36 Richard Saltus, "Genetic Clairvoyance," *Boston Globe Sunday Magazine*, January 8, 1995.

37 Saltus, "Clairvoyance."

38 "Genetic Testing Reviewed by Congress," *Science and Technology in Congress*, September, 1998 (American Association for the Advancement of Science, 1998) retrieved from http://www.aaas.org/spp/dspp/cstc/bulletin/articles/5-99/gentest.htm

39 "Regulatory Developments in Genetic Testing in the United States," Organization for Economic Co-Operation and Development, retrieved from http://www.oecd.org/EN/document/0,EN-document-617-1-no-21-22460-617,FF.html.

40 "Ensuring the Safe and Appropriate Use of Genetic Tests," U.S. Department of Health and Human Services, HHS Fact Sheet, January 29, 2001, retrieved from http://www.hhs.gov/news/press/2001pres/01fsgenetictests.html.

41 "Position Statement on Gene Patents and Accessibility of Gene Testing," American College of Medical Genetics, retrieved from http://www.faseb.org/genetics/acmg/pol-34.htm.

42 "Tragic Testing," *GeneWatch* 16, no. 3, (May-June 2003).

43 Janlori Goldman, Zoe Hudson and Richard Smith, "Privacy: Report on the Privacy Policies and Practices of Health Web Sites," *American Association for the Advancement of Science Professional Ethics Report*, November 9, 2000 at www.aaas.org.

44 A British company has designed a genetic test for cystic fibrosis that can be completed at home. The patient spits into a test tube and sends it through the mail to the company. "Tests Can Cost up to Pounds 1,500," *The Times (London)*, December 14, 1998.

45 Goldman, Hudson and Smith, "Privacy."

46 Dave Amber, "Oversight of Genetic Testing: Report Recommends More Government Control," *The Scientist* 14 (15), (July 24, 2000): 24.

47 "Genetic Testing: Addressing the Benefits and Challenges," *U.S. Department of Health and Human Services Fact Sheet*, January 12, 2000.

48 Margaret M. McGovern, "Laboratory Accreditation," Abstract, from a paper given at *Organization for Economic Co-Operation and Development Workshop Vienna 2000 on Genetic Testing: Policy Issues for the New Millennium*, February, 2000.

49 "Genetic Testing for Breast Cancer Risk: It's Your Choice," retrieved from *CancerNet* at www.cancernet.nci.nih.gov., August 7, 2000

50 "Genetic Discrimination, A Position Paper Presented by: The Council for Responsible Genetics," retrieved from www.gene-watch.org/programs/index.html

51 *Prenatal Testing and Disability Rights*, ed. Erik Parens and Adrienne Asch (Washington, D.C.: Georgetown University Press, 2000), ix.

52 Parens and Asch, *Prenatal Testing*, 5.

53 Victor R. Grann, "Benefits and Costs of Genetic Testing: The Case of Breast Cancer," Abstract, from the *Organization for Economic Co-Operation and Development Workshop Vienna 2000 on Genetic Testing: Policy Issues for the New Millennium*, February, 2000.

54 *Gattaca*, writ. and dir. Andrew Niccol, Columbia Pictures, 1998.

55 Stephen Jay Gould, "Humbled by the Genome's Mysteries," *New York Times*, February 19, 2001.

56 Wilfred Funk, *Word Origins and Their Romantic Stories*, (New York, New York: Bell Publishing Company, 1978), 269.

57 Ruth Hubbard and Elijah Wald, *Exploding the Gene Myth*, (Cambridge, Massachusetts: Beacon Press, 1993), 50.

58 Evelyn Fox Keller, "Is There an Organism in This Text?" in *Controlling Our Destinies: Historical, Philosophical, Ethical, and Theological Perspectives on the Human Genome Project*, (Notre Dame, Indiana: University of Notre Dame Press, 2000), 274.

59 Arielle Emmett, "Environment vs. Genes," *The Scientist* 15 (16) (August 20, 2001): 10.

60 David J. Weatherall, "Single gene disorders or complex traits: lessons from the thalassaemias and other monogenic diseases," *BMJ* 321, (November 4, 2000): 1117-1120.

61 Paul Lichtenstein, Niels V. Holm, et.al., "Environmental and Heritable Factors in the Causation of Cancer – Analyses of Cohorts of Twins from Sweden, Denmark, and Finland," *The New England Journal of Medicine* 343, no. 2, (July 13, 2000).

62 Rick Weiss, "Cancer Study Deemphasizes Genes' Role: Environmental, Behavioral Factors Are Predominant," *The Washington Post*, July 13, 2000.

63 C. elegans only comes in two sexes: male and hermaphrodite. By default I have labeled it an "it." Its genetic make up also made it on the front page of the *New York Times*, February 13, 2001.

64 This statistic and most of the information on Mr. C. elegans was taken from Kenneth F. Schaffner's examination of the creature in Reduction and Determinism, *Controlling Our Destinies: Historical, Philosophical, Ethical, and Theological Perspectives on the Human Genome Project* (Notre Dame, Indiana: University of Notre Dame Press, 2000), 306-312. A graduate student in molecular biology corrected me and said,"Actually C.elegans is popular because it is genetically tractable and it has a precisely determined cell lineage." Whatever the reasons, the worm is popular.

65 Schaffner concentrates mostly on behavior that might be caused by the genetic make-up of the worm's nervous system, but he projects his argu-

ment to include physical conditions resulting from possible mutations in the nervous system such as cystic fibrosis.

66 Schaffner, 306.

67 Hubbard and Wald, 164.

68 Advertisement for Agilent Technologies, *New York Times*, September 1, 1999, B10.

69 Hubbard and Wald, 163.

70 Walter C. Willett, "Balancing Life-Style and Genomics Research for Disease Prevention," *Science* 296, (April 26, 2002): 695-696.

71 "Future of Gene Therapy Examined," Science & Technology in Congress, February 2000 retrieved from the American Association for the Advancement of Science web site at www.aaas.com.

72 Jesse did not die of gene therapy directly, but rather during experiments testing how normal or redesigned cells could be transferred into the body.

73 Michael Rubinkam, "Family of Gene Therapy Patient Agrees to Settlement," *Associated Press*, November 5, 2000.

74 "Future of Gene Therapy Examined," *Science and Technology in Congress*, report by American Association for the Advancement of Science, February, 2000 at www.aaas.com.

75 LeRoy Walters, "Statement Before the Subcommittee on Public Health, Senate Health and Education Committee," February 2, 2000, retrieved f   r   o   m http://www.senate.gov/~labor/hearings/feb00hrg/0s00s00wt/frist0202/gelsing/kast/patter/fda-zoon/verma/walters/walters.htm

76 "Institutional Review Boards: The Emergence of Independent Boards, Department of Health and Human Services," Office of the Inspector General, June 1998: OEI-01-97-00192

77 "Institutional Review Boards,": Department of Health and Human Services.

78 Rick Weiss, "U.S. Halts Research On Humans at Duke: University Can't Ensure Safety, Probers Find," *Washington Post*, May 12, 1999.

79 Lisa M. Krieger, "Genetic Researchers Cite Specter of Profits," *San Jose Mercury News*, February 17, 2000.

80 Dave Amber, "Oversight of Genetic Testing: Report Recommends More Government Control," *The Scientist* 14 (15), (July 24, 2000): 24.

81 "There Are Many Reasons Why People are Reluctant to Participate in Clinical Trials," *Health Care News* 2, Issue 7, (March 26, 2002).

82 Michael Kranish, "Breakthroughs in Effort to Map Body's Proteins," *Boston Globe*, February 6, 2002.

83 Kranish, "Breakthroughs."

84 The financial interest in proteomics may be gone already for investors: "We've talked to analysts on Wall Street and they're sick and tired of hearing the word 'proteomics," Michael Becker, the investor relations officer at Cytogen Corp, told *The Scientist*. Susan Warner, "Once Promising Proteomics Market Sags," *The Scientist* 16[8], (April 15, 2002): 18.

85 Already, gene therapy is being marketed again in news shows and newspaper stories. While the scientists talk about the amazing promises of their technology, they say little about what protections have been added that will protect the patients in the test. See Paul Elias, "Gene Therapy," for an example.

CHAPTER FOUR

1 Submission in Response to Revised Interim Guidelines for Examination of Patent Applications under the 35 U.S.C. sec, 112 issued in the Federal Register 64 FR 71,427 on December 21, 1999, Comment 40, Submitting Parties: Michael Finney on behalf of MJ Research, Inc.

2 "2000 Gene Patents and other Genomic Inventions," Hearing before the Subcommittee on Courts and Intellectual Property of the Committee on the Judiciary House of Representatives, 106th Congress, Second Session, July 13, 2000. Serial No. 121

3 Thanks to Warren Kaplan, an intellectual property lawyer, for fleshing out some of the workings of the PTO

4 Gary Walsh, *Biopharmaceuticals: Biochemistry and Biotechnology*, (New York, New York: John Wiley & Sons, 1999), 51.

5 *Diamond vs. Chakrabarty*, 447 U.S. 303, 313 (1980).

6 Clearly, the hand of woman has played a part as well., though it is perhaps statistically correct that we lay the majority of blame for the very idea of life patents on men.

7 *Amgen Inc. v. Chugai Pharmaceutical Company*, 927 F. 2d 1200 (Federal Circuit 1991).

8 United States Patent and Trademark Office, Utility Examination Guidelines, January 5, 2001 (Volume 66, Number 4), retrieved from the Federal Register Online via GPO Access at wais.access.gpo.gov.

9 "Oversight Hearing on Gene Patents and Other Genomic Inventions," July 13, 2000, 89.

10 Submission in Response to Revised Interim Guidelines for Examination of Patent Applications under the 35 U.S.C. sec, 112 issued in the Federal Register 64 FR 71,427 on December 21, 1999, Comment 40, Submitting Parties: Michael Finney on behalf of MJ Research, Inc.

11 Submission in Response to Revised Interim Guidelines for Examination of Patent Applications under the 35 U.S.C. sec, 112 issued in the Federal

Register 64 FR 71,427 on December 21, 1999, Comment 40, Submitting Parties: Michael Finney on behalf of MJ Research, Inc.

12 "2000 Gene Patents and other Genomic Inventions," Hearing before the Subcommittee on Courts and Intellectual Property of the Committee on the Judiciary House of Representatives, 106th Congress, Second Session, July 13, 2000. Serial No. 121, 129.

13 "2000 Gene Patents and other Genomic Inventions," Hearing before the Subcommittee on Courts and Intellectual Property of the Committee on the Judiciary House of Representatives, 106th Congress, Second Session, July 13, 2000. Serial No. 121, Appendix, 157.

14 Paul Jacobs and Peter G. Gosselin, "'Robber Barons of the Genetic Age': Experts Fret Over Effect of Gene Patents on Reseaerch," *Los Angeles Times*, February 28, 2000.

15 Jacobs and Gosselin.

16 Warren A. Kaplan & Sheldon Krimsky, "Patentability of Biotechnology Inventions Under the PTO Utility Guidelines: Still Uncertain After All These Years?" *Journal of Biolaw and Business*, Intellectual Property, 2001.

17 Walter C. Willett, "Balancing Life-Style and Genomics Research for Disease Prevention," *Science* 296,(April 26, 2002): 695.

18 "Epogen FAQ," retrieved from the Amgen corporate web site: www.amgen.com.

19 "Myriad Genetics Reinforces its Strong Intellectual Property Position with the Award of Two More Patents in Breast Cancer," Myriad Press Release, April 25, 2000 retrieved from Myriad web page at http;//www.myriad.com/pr/20000425.html.

20 Stephen Herrera, "Epochal Drug: The House that EPO Built," *Red Herring Magazine*, May, 2000.

21 Andrew Pollack, "Two paths to the Same Protein," *New York Times* on the Web, March 28, 2000.

22 Rhonda L. Rundle, "Biotech Battlefront: Amgen Cleared to Sell Kidney-Patient Drug, Still faces Big Hurdles," *Wall Street Journal*, June 2, 1989.

23 Rundle, "Biotech Battlefront."

24 David Lawsky, "Nader Charges Amgen Won't Improve Drug Efficiency," *Reuters*, April 16, 2000.

25 Lawsky, "Nader."

26 "Outcome of Amgen Suit Could Affect Entire Biotech Industry," *Los Angeles Times*, June 4, 2000.

27 "Outcome of Amgen Suite Could Affect Entire Biotech Industry," *Los Angeles Times*, June 4, 2000.

28 Angela Zimm, "Amgen Rises on Court Win; Rival Transkaryotic Drops," retrieved from Bloomberg.com, on January 22, 2001.

29 Fred Warshofsky, *The Patent Wars: The Battle to Own the World's Technology* (New York, New York: John Wiley & Sons, 1994), 223.

30 Rochelle K. Seide & Janet M. MacLeod, "Drafting Claims for Biotechnological Inventions," 585 PLI/Pat. 381, 388 n. 10 (1999).

31 Vandana Shiva, "North-South Conflicts in Intellectual Property Rights," *Peace Review* 12:4 (2000): 504.

32 Leon R. Kass, *Toward a More Natural Science*, (New York, New York: The Free Press, 1985), 152.

33 Vandana Shiva, "Democratizing Biology," *Reinventing Biology: Respect for Life and the Creation of Knowledge*, (Indianapolis, Indiana: Indiana University Press, 1995), 68.

34 Ruth Hubbard and Sheldon Krimsky, "The Patented Mouse," *GeneWatch*, Vol. 5, No. 1, published by the Council for Responsible Genetics.

35 Ani DiFranco, "My I.Q.," from the album *Puddle Jump,* (Righteous Babe Music,/BMI, 1993).

36 "Report of the National Institutes of Health (NIH) Working Group on Research Tools, " Presented to the Advisory Committee to the Director, June 4, 1998.

37 Eliot Marshall, "The Mouse that Prompted a Roar," *Science* 277, (July 4, 1997).

38 Karyn Hede George, "Broad Research-Tool Patents: Boon or Burden?" *The Journal of NIH Research* 8, (January 1996).

39 "Sterile Harvest: New Crop of Terminator Patents Threatens Food Sovereignty, ETC Group, News Release, January 31, 2002, retrieved from www.etcgroup.org, February 11, 2002.

40 Christopher May, *A Global Economy of Intellectual Property Rights: The New Enclosures?* (New York, New York: Routledge, 2000), 104.

41 "2001: A Seed Odyssey, Suicide Seeds: Not Dead Yet!" *RAFI Communiqué,* Jan/Feb 2001, Issue #68.

42 "Sterile Harvest," January 31, 2002.

43 "Not Dead Yet!" *RAFI Communiqué*.

44 "Sterile Harvest," January 31, 2002.

45 "Not Dead Yet!" *RAFI Communiqué*

46 "Toxic Secret," CBSNews.com, November 10, 2002, retrieved from http://www.cbsnews.com

47 "Anniston, Alabama: In-Depth Pollution, Contamination, Betrayal," January 11, 2002, Environmental Working Group, retrieved from http://www.ewg.org/reports/anniston/

48 Bill McKibben, *The End of Nature*, (New York, New York: Random House, 1989), 167.

49 Barry S. Edwards, "'...and on his farm he had a geep': Patenting Transgenic Animals," *Minnesota Intellectual Property Review*, 89 (Vol. 2, Number 1, 2001), 91.

50 Edwards, 91.

51 *Lowell v. Lewis*, 15 F. Cas. 1018, 1019 (D. Mass.1817) (No. 8568) cited in Edwards, 111.

52 "2000 Gene Patents and other Genomic Inventions," Hearing before the Subcommittee on Courts and Intellectual Property of the Committee on the Judiciary House of Representatives, 106th Congress, Second Session, July 13, 2000. Serial No. 121

53 Karyn Hede George, "Broad Research-Tool Patents: Boon or Burden," *The Journal of NIH Research*, January 1996, Vol. 8, p. 29.

54 "2000 Gene Patents and other Genomic Inventions," Hearing before the Subcommittee on Courts and Intellectual Property, 39.

55 "Broad Coalition Challenges Patents on Life," Community Nutrition Institute, June 6, 1995, retrieved from http://www.rz.uni-frankfurt.de/~ecstein/gen/biolib/320

56 Martin Khor, "A Worldwide Fight Against Biopiracy and Patents on Life," Third World Network, retrieved from http://twnside.org

57 *Chakrabarty* 447 U.S. at 318, cited in Edwards, 112.

58 The title of a book on genetically modified foodstuffs. Martin Teitel and Kimberly A. Wilson, *Genetically Engineered Food: Changing the Nature of Nature*, (Boston, MA: Park Street Press, 1999).

CHAPTER FIVE

1 "Genentech Congressional Testimony Addresses Broader Patent Issues," Genentech press release, July 13, 2000, retrieved from www.genentech.com. Levinson did, however, support the new utility guidelines for patent applications that the Patent Office subsequently published in January, 2001.

2 William Greider, *Who Will Tell the People?* (New York, New York: Simon & Schuster, 1992), 58.

3 David D. Lee, "Herbert Hoover and the Golden Age of Aviation," in *Aviation's Golden Age: Portraits from the 1920's and 1930's*, ed. William M. Leary, (Iowa City, Iowa: University of Iowa Press, 1989), 136.

4 Glenn E. Bugos, "The History of the Aerospace Industry." EH.Net Encyclopedia, ed. Robert Whaples, August 29, 2001 retrieved from www.eh.net/encyclopedia/contents, February 7, 2002.

5   Bill Robie, *For the Greatest Achievement: A History of the Aero Club of America and the National Aeronautic Association*, (Washington, D.C.: Smithsonian Institution Press, 1993), Chapters 6, 8, and 11.

6   Robie, 94-95.

7   Lee, 128.

8   Lee, 136.

9   Lee, 136.

10 Lee, 93.

11 "Patent History," BountyQuest web site, retrieved from www.bountyquest.com/patent/patenthistory.htm February 8, 2002.

12 "Patent History," BountyQuest.

13 Arthur R. Miller and Michael H. Davis, *Intellectual Property: Patents, Trademarks, and Copyright In a Nutshell*, (St. Paul, Minnesota: West Group, 2000) 18, 19.

14 "Gene Patents and Other Genomic Inventions" Hearing Before the Subcommittee on Courts and Intellectual Property of the Committee on the Judiciary House of Representatives, 106th Congress, Second Session, July 13, 2000, 82. Retrieved from http://commdocs.house.gov/committees/judiciary/hju66043.000/hju66043_0.htm

15 "Drugs Ex Machina," *The Economist*, September 22, 2001. See also Peter Tollman, Philippe Guy, Jill Altshuler, Alastair Flanagan, Michael Steiner, "A Revolution in R&D: How Genomics and Genetics are Transforming the Biopharmaceutical Industry," The Boston Consulting Group, November 2001.

16 Lisa Ruby Basara and Michael Montagne, *Searching for Magic Bullets: Orphan Drugs, Consumer Activism, and Pharmaceutical Development*, (New York, New York: Pharmaceutical Products Press, 1994), 8.

17 Brian O'Reilly, "There's Still Gold in Them Thar Pills," *Fortune*, July 23, 2001 and Lee Clifford, Brian O'Keefe, and David Stires, "A New Prescription for Your Portfolio," *Fortune*, July 23, 2001.

18 Alice Dembner, "Public Handouts Enrich Drug Makers, Scientists," *The Boston Globe*, April 5, 1998.

19 O'Reilly, "Gold," 70.

20 Lisa Meyer, Stock Screen: "Biotech to Bank On," *Red Herring*, February 22, 2001 and David Malakoff and Robert F. Service, "Genomania Meets the Bottom Line," *Science* 291, (February 16, 2001): 1201.

21 "Climbing the Helical Staircase," *The Economist*, March 27, 2003. See also, Naomi Aoki, "Midsize Biotech Firms Take Hit," *The Boston Globe*, June 10, 2002.

22 Andrew Pollack, "Biotechnology Seeks End to Slump," *The New York Times*, May 19, 2002.

23 "Climbing the Helical Staircase," *The Economist*, March 27, 2003.

24 Note the example of the biotechnology company ImClone. After 17 years in existence and spending $200 million, it still had not turned a profit. The research on the company's "blockbuster" cancer drug Erbitux was deemed inadequate by the FDA in December of 2001, resulting in a myriad of financial scandals. At the core was a biotechnology company desperate to produce product and as quickly as possible. Catherine Arnst, "Where ImClone Went Wrong," *Business Week Online*, February 18, 2002 retrieved from http://www.businessweek.com.

25 Peter Tollman, Philippe Guy, Jill Altshuler, Alastair Flanagan, Michael Steiner, "A Revolution in R&D: How Genomics and Genetics are Transforming the Biopharmaceutical Industry," The Boston Consulting Group, November 2001.

26 Susan Warner, "Once Promising Proteomics Market Sags," *The Scientist*, 16[8]:18, April 15, 2002.

27 "Coming of Age," *The Economist*, December 22, 2001, 80.

28 Andrew Pollack, "The Genome is Mapped. Now He Wants Profit," *The New York Times*, February 24, 2002.

29 O'Reilly, 66.

30 The low figure is found in *Pharmaceutical R & D: Costs, Risks and Rewards*, Office of Technology Assessment, U.S. Congress (Washington, DC: U.S. Government Printing Office, February, 1993). The higher figure is used in *A Revolution in R&D: How Genomics and Genetics are Transforming the Biopharmaceutical Industry*, The Boston Consulting Group, November 2001.

31 *Pharmaceutical R & D: Costs, Risks and Rewards*, Office of Technology Assessment, U.S. Congress (Washington, DC: U.S. Government Printing Office, February, 1993).

32 There is a question of whether the cost to bring new drugs to market also includes basic research that was paid for by the public. The International Society for Ecology and Culture has estimated that "three-quarters of American industrial patents in recent years were based on research financed by the public." Steven Gorelick, "Research: Who Pays, Who Profits?" in *Small is Beautiful, Big is Subsidized*, The International Society for Ecology and Culture, (Devon, U.K: The Devonshire Press, 1998), 32.

33 James Love, "Call for More Reliable Costs Data on Clinical Trials," January 13, 1997, first published in *Marketletter*, January 13, 1997, retrieved from http://cptech.org/pharm/marketletter.html

34 "Drugs Ex Machina."

35 Tollman, et.al., 6.

36 Lisa Ruby Basara and Michael Montagne, *Searching for Magic Bullets: Orphan Drugs, Consumer Activism, and Pharmaceutical Development*, (Binghampton, NY: Pharmaceutical Products Press, 1994), 173.

37 "Ten Year Financial Summary," Bristol-Myers Squibb Company web site, retrieved from www.bms.com/lannding/data/index.html.

38 Big pharmaceutical companies can also pay off generic companies so they won't bring competitive drugs to market. Community Catalyst, a consumer coalition, accuses three name-brand companies of paying millions to generic drug companies if they would keep from producing the generic version of a drug that is used by thousands of people along with medications for high blood pressure. Liz Kowalczyk, "Consumer Group Sues Three Drug Makers," *The Boston Globe*, June 8, 2001.

39 Jesse Eisinger, "Roche's Planned Job Cuts Look Desperate, Not Smart," *The Wall Street Journal*, June 1, 2001.

40 Stephen S. Hall, "Prescription for Profit," *The New York Times Magazine*, March 11, 2001, 40.

41 Report of the National Institutes of Health (NIH) Working Group on Research Tools, "Presented to the Advisory Committee to the Director, June 4, 1998.

42 Rhonda L. Rundle, "Biotech Battlefront: Amgen Cleared to Sell Kidney-Patient Drug, Still faces Big Hurdles," *Wall Street Journal*, June 2, 1989.

43 Jean O. Lanjouw and Josh Lerner, "The Enforcement of Intellectual Property Right: A Survey of the Empirical Literature," National Bureau of Economic Research. Working Paper 6296, December 1997, retrieved from www.nber.org/papers/w6296, 8.

44 Jean O. Lanjouw and Josh Lerner, "The Enforcement of Intellectual Property Rights: A Survey of the Empirical Literature," National Bureau of Economic Research, Working Paper 6296, December 1997, retrieved from www.nber.org/papers/w6296, 8.

45 Brenda Sandburg, "A New Industry Transforms the Patent System," *The Recorder*, July 31, 2001, retrieved from law.com on February 17, 2002.

46 David Malakoff, "Will a Smaller Genome Complicate the Patent Chase?" *Science_291*, (February 16, 2001): 1194.

47 "Climbing the Helical Staircase," *The Economist*, March 27, 2003.

48 Lanjouw, et.al., 16.

49 Lanjouw, et.al., 17.

50 Fred Warshofsky, *The Patent Wars: The Battle to Own the World's Technology*, (New York: John Wiley & Sons, Inc., 1994), 247, 248.

51 Jean O. Lanjouw and Mark Schankerman, "Stylized Facts of Patent Litigation: Value, Scope and Ownership," National Bureau of Economic Research, Working Paper 6297, December, 1997, retrieved from www.nber.org/papers/w6297, 10.

52 Brenda Sandburg, "Battling the Patent Trolls," *The Recorder*, July 31, 2001, retrieved from law.com on February 17, 2002.

53 Jean O. Lanjouw and Josh Lerner, "The Enforcement of Intellectual Property Rights: A Survey of the Empirical Literature," National Bureau of Economic Research, Working Paper 6296, December 1997, retrieved from www.nber.org/papers/w6296, 1

54 Donald H. Dalton and Manuel G. Serapio, "Globalizing Industrial Research and Development," U.S. Department of Commerce, Technology Administration, September 1999, 47.

55 Dalton and Serapio, 50.

56 William Greider, *One World, Ready or Not*, (New York, New York: Simon & Schuster, 1997).

57 Brian O'Reilly, "There's Still Gold in Them Thar Pills," *Fortune,* July 23, 2001, 61.

58 Dalton and Serapio, 5.

59 Dalton and Serapio, 5.

60 William Greider, *One World Ready or Not: The Manic Logic of Global Capitalism*, (New York, New York: Simon & Schuster, 1997), 25.

CHAPTER SIX

1   Charles Miller, *Jefferson and Nature: An Interpretation*, (Baltimore, Maryland: The Johns Hopkins University Press, 1988), 220.

2   Silvo A. Bedini, *Thomas Jefferson: Statesman of Science*, (New York, New York: Macmillan Publishing Co., 1990), 209.

3   Curtis, William Eleroy, *The True Thomas Jefferson*, (Philadelphia, Pennsylvania: J.B. Lippincott Company, 1901), 374-382.

4   To James Madison, July 31, 1788. *The Life and Selected Writings of Thomas Jefferson*, ed. Adrienne Koch & William Peden (New York, New York: The Modern Library, Random House, 1944), 451.

5   Koch and Peden, 450-451.

6   Curtis, 381.

7   Subsequently, someone else took out a patent on the stove Franklin invented and, according to him, made "a little Fortune by it." Franklin, Benjamin, *The Autobiography and Other Writings* (New York, New York: Penguin Books, 1986), 130.

8 Charles Miller, *Jefferson and Nature: An Interpretation*, (Baltimore, Maryland: The Johns Hopkins University Press, 1988), 203.

9 See Sheryl Gay Stolberg, "Patent on Human Stem Cell Puts U.S. Officials in Bind," *New York Times*, August 17, 2001.

10 Ronald Kotulak, "Patents are University Gold Mine," *Chicago Tribune*, December 9, 2001.

11 Lor Andrews, "Embryo Decision Raises New Issues," *Newsday.com*, August 13, 2001, retrieved from www.newsday.com on August 29, 2001.

12 Sheryl Gay Stolberg, "Patent Laws May Determine Shape of Stem Cell Research," *The New York Times*, August 17, 2001.

13 Ronald Kotulak, "Patents are University Gold Mine," *Chicago Tribune*, December 9, 2001.

14 Andrews.

15 Sheryl Gay Stolberg, "Patent Laws."

16 Sheryl Gay Stolberg, "Suit Seeks to Expand Access to Stem Cells," *The New York Times*, August14, 2001.

17 Paul Elias, "Geron Narrows Stem-Cell Focus," *Associated Press*, January 10, 2002.

18 Ronald Schapira, "Biotechnology Patents in the United States," *Biotechnology, Patents, and Morality*, ed. Sigrid Sterckx, (Adershot, U.K.: Ashgate, 1997), 172.

19 Singer, Joseph William, *The Edges of the Field: Lessons on the Obligations of Ownership*, (Boston, Massachusetts: Beacon Press, 2000), 87.

CHAPTER SEVEN

1 Sheldon Rampton and John Stauber, *Trust Us, We're Experts: How Industry Manipulates Science and Gambles with Your Future*, (New York, New York: Jeremy P. Tacher/Putnam, 2001), 302.

2 "CBHD Denounces Patenting of Human Cloning," The Center for Bioethics and Human Dignity Home Page retrieved from http://www.cbhd.org/media/pr/pr2002-05-16.htm

3 Andrew Pollack, "Debate on Human Cloning Turns to Patents," *The New York Times*, May 17, 2002.

4 Andrew Pollack, "Debate on Human Cloning."

5 "Human Embryo Cloning Patent Challenged," *Environment News Service*, March 30, 2000, retrieved on from http://ens.lycos.com/ens/mar2000/2000L-03-30-02.html.

6 "It might just be that you just can't make humans this way," Taja Dominko of the biotechnology company Advanced Cell Technology (ACT) told a medical conference in 2001. Quoted in "Testimony of Andrew Kimbrell,

Executive Director Internnational Center for Technology Assessment given before the Senate Judiciary Committee Feinstein Hearing," retrieved from from IBC home page.

7   Rifkin and Newman have appealed.

8   Jehanne Henry, "Biotech's Bad Boy: Jeremy Rifkin is trying to make a monkey out of the biotech business," *California Lawyer*, November 1999, 53.

9   Andrew Pollack, "Debate on Human Cloning Turns to Patents," *The New York Times*, May 17, 2002. Italics mine.

10   "Bankrupt BioTransplant Handed Delisting Notice," March 4, 2003, *Boston Business Journal*, retrieved from www.bizjournals.com/boston/stories/2003/03/03/daily14.html

11   Robert M. Goldberg, "The War Against Cipro," *National Review Online*, October 25, 2001, retrieved from www.nationalreview.com/comment, February 11, 2002.

12   "Journal of the State Convention," (Jackson, MS: E. Barksdale, State Printer, 1861), 86—88.

13   Quoted in Holmes Rolston, III, *Genes, Genesis and God*, (Cambridge, England: Cambridge University Press, 1999), 27.

14   *Abrams v. United States*, 630-31, quoted in Louis Menand, *The Metaphysical Club*, (New York, New York: Farrar, Straus and Giroux, 2001),430.

15   Seth Shulman, Toward Sharing the Genome, *Technology Review: MIT's Magazine of Innovation*, September/October 2000.

16   Lynn Rivers, "Patents Undermine Promise of Genetic Revolution," retrieved from www.hillnews.com/061902/ss.rivers aspx

17   Rivers, see also Rebecca Charnas, "'No Patents on Life' Working Group Update," retrieved from Council of Responsible Genetics web site at www.gene-watch.org.

Index

About the Author

Matthew Albright lives in Durango, Colorado. His articles on ethics and the human body have appeared in *Z Magazine*, *CounterPunch.org*, *GeneWatch*, and *Psychoanalysis and Contemporary Culture*. He holds degrees from the University of Southern California and the College of Santa Fe and recently completed his Master of Divinity at Harvard University. He also holds the record in *The Guinness Book of World Records* for the longest softball game, 1986: 104 hours.